COLLECTORS EDITION

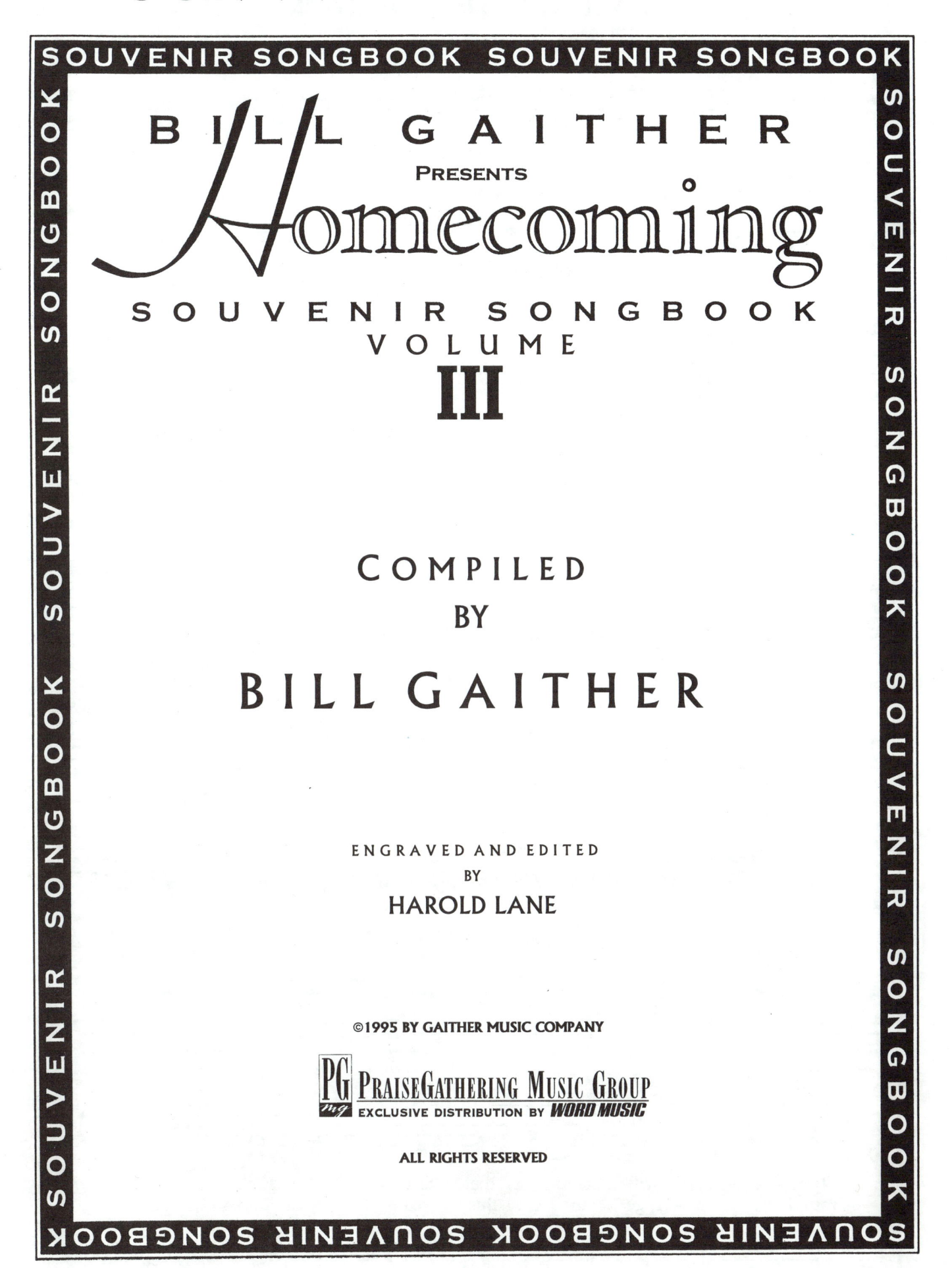

BILL GAITHER
Presents
Homecoming
SOUVENIR SONGBOOK
VOLUME
III

COMPILED BY
BILL GAITHER

ENGRAVED AND EDITED
BY
HAROLD LANE

©1995 BY GAITHER MUSIC COMPANY

PG **PraiseGathering Music Group**
EXCLUSIVE DISTRIBUTION BY **WORD MUSIC**

ALL RIGHTS RESERVED

Gaither Music
COMPANY

Lead Me To The Rock

S.W.M.

Sheldon Wade Mencer

1. When I'm tossed up-on life's sea and the old waves trou-ble me, When it seems that there's no re-fuge I can find, Well, I know where there's a place, It's a hav-en of sweet rest, A might-y Tow-er that will stand the test of time.

2. So, I will not be a-fraid, nor will I be dis-mayed, for He hides me in the hol-low of His hand; There is noth-ing that can harm me, There is noth-ing to a-larm me for I've found a re-fuge in this wea-ry land.

© Copyright 1987 by Sheldon Wade Publishing. All rights reserved. Used by permission of Gaither Copyright Management.

Lead me to the Rock. Lead me to the Rock. He's the Rock of my sal-va-tion, a sure and firm Foun-da-tion, Je-sus is the Rock on which I stand, All oth-er ground is sink-ing sand, Lead me to the Rock that is high-er than I.

Crown Him King

Luther G. Presley
Wallace Varner

1. The Sav-ior left His sweet home a-bove, came to re-deem by love, Won-der-ful heav'n-ly Dove, just think how He loved us, Dy-ing up-on the cross, bear-ing the pain and loss,
2. No more in bond-age of sin we roam, light has dis-pelled the gloam, With Him we're fac-ing home, Close to our side each day, cheer-ing a-long the way, What a great Sav-ior is
3. Let ev-'ry heart His great name a-dore, prais-ing Him more and more, For the cross that He bore, how_____ Will-ing to die a-lone, for our sins to a-tone,

CHORUS

He, our great and match-less Sav-ior. Sing His prais-es, Sing sing His prais-es, Bow be-fore___ Him, mag-ni-
praise His prais-es, and bless His name,

© Copyright 1945 Stamps Baxter Music. All rights reserved. Used by permission of Benson Music Group, Inc.

Cm Bb F7 F7/C F° F7 F° F7 F° F7 F° F7
fy His name, Let the whole world, let the whole world
Let all the world
F7
His love pro-claim all ye peo-ple;
For-ev-er, and for-ev-er, praise Him with joy, all ye peo-ple;
Bb Bb+ Bb6 Bb+ Bb6 Bb6 Bb
Sing His prais-es, sing His prais-es, And His
Sing His praise, His name
Bb7/D Eb E°
great name, bless-ed name a-dore, Crown Him crown Him,
a-dore, Crown Him,
Bb/F Gb7 Bb/F Bb/D C F7 Bb
crown Him, crown Him, King for-ev-er, ev-er-more.
crown Him, King for-ev-er-more.

When Morning Sweeps The Eastern Sky

O. A. P.
O. A. Parris

1. Christ is coming back to reign upon the earth again, The saints are looking forward to the morning by and by; We will have no Satan then, no sorrows, tears or pain, When morning dawn sweeps across the eastern sky.

2. This old world is reeling with its load of sin and greed, The saints are looking for the glory morning by and by; From their tribulations all God's children will be freed, When dawns the morning in the eastern sky.

3. I'll be in the rapture with the ones who are set free, The saints are looking for the morning by and by; What a happy meeting, what a mighty jubilee, When morning dawn eternal sweeps across the eastern sky.

(Bass) Saints are looking for the morning by and by; When the morning sweeps across the eastern sky.

© Copyright 1973 Stamps Quartet Music. All rights reserved. Used by permission of Integrated Copyright Group, Inc.

CHORUS
D♭ D♭/F D♭ B♭°
Oh, hap-py day when the glo - ry morn-ing sweeps the
Hap - py day, in the
Oh, hap-py day when the glo-ry morn-ing sweeps the
Oh, hap-py day in glo - ry when the morn-ing sweeps the
D♭/F D♭ A♭
sky, I'll bid the sor-rows of this world good - by;
sky, I'll bid the world and its sor - rows good - by;
sky, I'll bid the world and its cares good - by;
sky, Bid the world good - by;
N.C. D♭ G♭/D♭ D♭ G♭/D♭ D♭ D♭/F A♭
Saints that are here will be caught up in the
Saints that are here will be caught up in - to the
Oh, hal - le - lu - jah, The saints that are here will meet in the
Saints down here will fly a-way in the
D♭ D♭/A♭ D♭/F A♭7/E♭ D♭/A♭ D♭
air, When morn-ing sweeps a - cross the east-ern sky.
air, When morn-ing sweeps the east - ern sky.
air, When morn-ing sweeps the east - ern sky.
air, When morn-ing sweeps the east - ern sky.

I Am Not Ashamed

D. T.

Dawn Thomas

1. We're an anchor for those who are hurting. We're a harbor for those who are lost. Sometimes it's not always easy bearing Calvary's cross. We've been ridiculed by those who don't know Him, and mocked by those who don't believe. Still, I love standing

© Copyright 1989 McSpadden Music. All rights reserved. Used by permission of Integrated Copyright Group, Inc.

up for my Jesus 'cause of all that He's done for me.
That's why I am not ashamed of the gospel, the
gospel of Jesus Christ. No, I am not afraid
to be counted, I'm willing to give my life.
Now, I'm ready to be all He wants me to be:

E♭maj7
3
A♭9
B♭/F
give up the wrong for the right.
Oh no, I am not a -
3
Cm/F
B♭/F
shamed of the gos - pel, I am not a - shamed of the
Cm7/F
F7
1. B♭
on to verse II
2. B♭
FINE
gos - pel of Je - sus Christ.
Christ.
verse II
B♭
2. For ev - 'ry mo - ment His hand has had mer - cy, for all the
E♭maj9/7
A♭9
Gm
love He's shown all my life, A sim - ple 'thanks' does - n't

C9 F7sus F7
say how I'm feel - in', I get tears in my eyes. So as for
B♭
me, I'm gon - na keep on be - liev - in' in the
E♭maj9/7 A♭9 Gm7
3
One who's been so faith - ful to me. I'm not out to please this
D.S. al FINE
C9 C7 F7 E♭/F F7
3
whole world a - round me, I've got my mind on e - ter - ni - ty. That's why

Bigger Than Any Mountain

G. J.
Gordon Jensen

CHORUS

Bigger than all my problems; Bigger than all my fears; God is bigger than any mountain that I can or cannot see. Bigger than all my questions; Bigger than anything; God is bigger than any mountain that I can or cannot see.

FINE

© Copyright 1976 Jensen Music. All rights reserved. Used by permission of Benson Music Group, Inc.

1. Bigger than all the shadows that fall across my path;
2. Bigger than all the giants of fear and unbelief;

God is bigger than any mountain that I can or cannot see;

Bigger than all my confusion,
Bigger than all my hangups,

Bigger than anything; God is bigger than any mountain that I can or cannot see.

(2nd time: D.C. al FINE)

When We All Get Together With The Lord

1. Now when the rich and the poor get to-geth-er with the Lord,
2. Now when the tall and the small get to-geth-er with the Lord,

Get to-geth-er, get to-geth-er with the Lord,

Well, they will treat each oth-er like sis-ter and broth-er,
Well, then the weak are no long-er a-fraid of the strong-er,

When they all get to-geth-er with the Lord.

CHORUS

Now when they all get to-geth-er, When they
Praise God! Hal - le - lu - jah!

all get to-geth-er with the Lord,_____ Well, they will treat each oth-er like sis-ter and broth-er, when they all get to-geth-er with the Lord._____ Well, God has no fav-'rites and we're all the same, they say, We'll see our man-y friends and our loved ones on that day, We'll all be so hap-py when Saint

Peter leads the way, Then we'll sing, sing, sing, sing, sing; Now when they all get together, When they all get together with the Lord, Well, they will treat each other like sister and brother, when they all get together with the Lord, with the Lord.

I'M SO GLAD
I'M A PART
OF THE
FAMILY OF GOD.

Bill and Gloria Gaither

New Gaither videos trigger smiles, tears

Artists thrilled to return to Alexandria for sneak preview

BY BARBARA BAKER
Staff Correspondent

ALEXANDRIA—Bill Gaither was like a kid showing off new toys to his friends this week.

His new "toys" were the videos he had just finished, and his friends were singing in the videos. They had gathered from far and near at Gaither Studios in Alexandria in June to record three videos, "All Day Singing and Dinner on the Grounds," "Revival" and "Holy Ground."

This week, with many of his friends returning, Gaither let them have a sneak preview of themselves - even before the videos were released. They had just finished mixing them on Monday, said Lana Ranahan, manager of the studio.

As the group of singers viewed excerpts from two of the videos, it was apparent they were enjoying themselves. The expressions on friends as they greeted each other with hugs and grins.

"Be uninhibited," urged Gaither of the group, eager to capture their natural expressions on camera. Following a rehearsal on Monday evening, they continued recording Tuesday and Wednesday.

Present at the gathering were such Southern gospel singers as the Cathedrals, the Talleys and the Speers. One special, first timer to the group was Joni Eareckson Tada.

Gaither is featuring older singers as well as premiering new ones, said Ranahan. Norman Wood, who sang in the Dixie Four Quartet in Indianapolis in the 1940s and '50s, was there from St. Louis.

"I think Bill Gaither kind of grew up on the Dixie Four," said Wood. This was Wood's first time to join the group at Gaither Studios.

Gaither acknowledged the widow of Rosie Rozell, Betty Rozell, with expressions of love and comfort. Rosie had been present at

Providing the entertainment: Bill Gaither smiles his approval as Carl Erskine, Hall of Fame Major League Pitcher from the Brooklyn Dodgers, plays the harmonica during a gospel video session at Gaither Studios. (Perry Reichanadter photo)

Gaither Music video collection 'very rewarding'

their faces, shouts of joy, applause and at least two standing ovations proved their satisfaction. Gaither, who said he had been crying (for joy) and shouting while he had been editing the footage for six months, smiled broadly.

The singers had come once again this week to Gaither Studios to record two more videos that are yet to be named.

"They came from everywhere," said Ranahan. And it was evident they were happy to return and to be reunited with so many the last such recording. Singer Jake Hess told how Rosie, unable to walk before his recent death, expected to be at the taping at Gaither Studios.

"He's not here, but he's walking," declared Hess of his confidence that Rosie is in Heaven.

"All Day Singing and Dinner on the Grounds" and "Revival" will be ready in a couple of weeks, said Ranahan. "Holy Ground" is expected to be released in the fall.

Vestal Goodman performs as part of the Gaither Collection Video Series for Gaither Music Company.

REPRINTED WITH PERMISSION FROM THE HERALD BULLETIN

Hovie puttin' the hammer down

Dony McGuire with Bill

Fellowship

Doug & Naomi Sego Reader

Bill & Theta Hall (John's wife)

A new quartet

I don't know what this is

Boys will be boys

Jim Hill & Doug

Advice for Mark

Hovie scratching up my car

Frick & Frack

Boundless Love

Dianne Wilkinson   Dianne Wilkinson

1. There is not a mother, sister, friend or brother ___ loves the way that Jesus can; He proved His love for me when He died on Cal-va-ry, He ___ gave His life for fall-en ___ man.
2. Je-sus wants to love you, there is none a-bove you, ___ you are pre-cious in His sight; ___ He will nev-er fail you ___ when the doubts as-sail you, ___ He'll be with you day and ___ night.

CHORUS

His love ___ is a bound-less ___ love, and it reach-es down and touch-es ___ me; ___ His love ___ is an end-less ___ love

D.S. that will last through all e-ter-ni-ty.

© Copyright 1986 Homeward Bound Music. All rights reserved. Used by permission of Integrated Copyright Group, Inc.

Moving Up To Gloryland

Lee Roy Abernathy / Lee Roy Abernathy

1. I love to think about a paradise somewhere beyond the blue, A mansion waiting in the distant skies may be next door to you; We'll go parading somewhere beyond the blue, the day I gave up sin,

2. I made my reservation long ago, the day I gave up sin, And when my mansion's ready, this I know: I'm gonna move right in; I have a vision

© Copyright 1946 by Abernathy Publishing, renewed 1974 by Abernathy Publishing.
All rights reserved. Used by permission of Integrated Copyright Group, Inc.

rad- ing through the dis- tant stars,_____ right down the
through the dis- tant stars, right down the Milk-
vi- sion of a hap- py place_____ where friends and
of a hap- py place where friends and loved

Milk- y Way,_____ The plan- ets, Ju- pi- ter and
y Way,_____ The plan- ets, Ju- pi- ter and
loved ones meet,_____ Right on the cor- ner of God's
ones meet,_____ Right on the cor- ner of God's

Nep- tune and Mars won't e- ven be half way!____
Nep- tune and Mars won't e- ven be half way!____
Av- e- nue and Hal- le- lu- jah Street!____
Av- e- nue and Hal- le- lu- jah Street!____

CHORUS

Mov- ing, mov- ing, mov- in up to
Oh, yes, I'm mov- ing, mov- ing, mov- ing, mov- ing,

C7 C13 F
D7
Glo - ry - land,
Mov - ing mov - ing,
Mov - ing, mov - ing, mov - ing, mov - ing,
F9
F7♭9 C7
F
D°
hold - ing to His nail - scarred hands;
Don't know when I'm leav - in' but I'm
C7 C° C7 C7/E
F6/A
A♭°
read - y to go;
When I get to Heav - en, I'll be
C7/G F♯° C7/G C7
F
D7
wel - come, I know,
Mov - ing, mov -
Mov - ing, mov - ing, mov - ing,
G7
C7 C13 F
ing, mov - ing up to Glo - ry - land.
mov - ing,

God Leads Us Along

G. A. Y.
G. A. Young

1. In shad-y, green pas-tures, so rich and so sweet, God leads His dear chil-dren a-long;___ Where the wa-ter's cool flow bathes the wea-ry one's feet, God leads His dear chil-dren a-long.__
2. Some-times on the mount where the sun shines so bright, God leads His dear chil-dren a-long;___ Some-times in the val-ley, in dark-est of night, God leads His dear chil-dren a-long.__
3. Though sor-rows be-fall us and e-vils op-pose, God leads His dear chil-dren a-long;___ Through grace we can con-quer, de-feat all our foes, God leads His dear chil-dren a-long.__

CHORUS

Some through the wa-ters, some through the flood, Some through the fire,___ but all through the blood;__ Some through great sor-row, but God gives a song, In the night sea-son and all the day long.

The Joy Of Heaven

Rupert Cravens
Elwood Denson

1. The joy of heav-en is swell-ing in my soul ev-'ry day, 'tis swell-ing, Sweet-er it grows to me and dai-ly o'er-flows; The love that saved me I'm tell-ing all a-long on my way, I'm glad for Je-sus' a-maz-ing grace to me, to me.

2. The joy of heav-en is giv-en by the Spir-it with-in, a-bid-ing, Grace to my heart so free-ly He doth im-part, And with my spir-it bears wit-ness that I'm saved from all sin, I'm glad for Je-sus' a-maz-ing grace to me, to me.

3. The joy of heav-en, like bil-lows, ev-er rolls on and on, in-creas-ing, Glo-ry so free 'tis ev-er bring-ing to me; This great sal-va-tion will keep me till life's morn-ing shall dawn, I'm glad for Je-sus' a-maz-ing grace to me, to me.

CHORUS

The joy of heav-en is ris-ing, swell-ing
The joy of heav'n It ris-es, swells
It gives me vic-t'ry o'er sin and e-vil
Gives vic-to-ry, o'er ev-'ry sin,

© Copyright 1950 (renewal 1977) my James D. Vaughan Music Publisher/SESAC, a div. of Pathway Music, P.O. Box 2250, Cleveland, TN 37320 in Morning Glory. Used by permission.

within my heart to ev-er surge and roll,
in my heart to ev-er surge and roll,
and ev-er floods my hap-py new-born soul;
And it floods my hap-py, new-born soul.

The lov-ing Sav-ior leads me by His Spir-it here,
Sav - ior

His love di-vine I see in ev-'ry place,
Love I see each place,

Oh, hal-le-lu-jah! Oh, glo-ry, glo-ry!
Oh, praise His name! I'm glad He came.

I praise the Lord for His a-maz-ing grace.
Praise Him for His grace.

The Happy Jubilee

Raymond Browning

Adger M. Pace

1. Praise the Lord, I've been in-vit-ed to a meet-ing in the air,
2. With the glo-ri-ous as-sem-bly dressed in gar-ments pure and white,
3. Sa-tan will be bound and wars will cease and Da-vid's Son will reign,

Ju-bi-lee! Ju-bi-lee! Ju-bi-lee! Ju-bi-lee!

All the saints of all the a-ges in their glo-ry will be there—
You will find me, for I'm watch-ing and my lamp is trimmed and bright—
All the ran-somed of the Lord shall come to Zi-on once a-gain,

Ju-bi-lee! Ju-bi-lee! Ju-bi-lee! Ju-bi-lee!

CHORUS

Ju-bi-lee! Ju-bi-lee! Ju-bi-lee! Ju-bi-lee! You're in-

© Copyright 1928, renewed 1956 Lillenas Publishing Co. All rights reserved. Used by permission.

vit - ed to that hap - py ju - bi - lee! _____ Ju - bi -

lee! _____ Ju - bi - lee! _____ Ju - bi - lee! _____ Ju - bi - lee! _____ You're in -

vit - ed to that hap - py ju - bi - lee!

Jackie Marshall

I'll Keep Walking In The King's Highway

Thomas Benton

Thomas Benton

1. I'll keep walk-ing in the King's high-way, 'tis the glo-ry road. Je-sus safe-ly leads me day by day, straight to the end-less a-bode. I'll be faith-ful and shall watch and pray, till I cease to roam. I'll keep walk-ing in the King's high-way till I reach home. Come walk with

2. I'll keep walk-ing in the light di-vine, safe with-in His love. I am sure the life crown will be mine, when I be-hold Him a-bove. Soon the end-less morn-ing will be-gin, bright e-ter-nal day. So with Him I'm go-ing home-ward in the King's high-way. Come a-long and walk with

Come and walk with

CHORUS

© Copyright 1931 Hartford Music Co. All rights reserved. Used by permission of Integrated Copyright Group, Inc.

Bbm Gbm/A Db/Ab
me on the King's
me and with Je - sus on the hap - py high - way,
me a - long the hap - py
Ab7 Db N.C.
high - way, on the shin - ing path to glo - ry.
hap - py King's high - way.
King's high - way.
Ab Ab/C Ab7 Db
O walk with Christ,
Walk with Je - sus, walk with, walk with Je - sus,
Won't you come and walk with
Db/F Dbm6/Fb Ab/Eb Eb Ab7
day by day, day by day;
walk with bless - ed Je - sus, day by day;
Je - sus ev - 'ry pass - ing day.
N.C. Db
Till a - bove we sing the sto - ry; Come
Come a - long and
Come and

28

walk with me and His
walk with me and with Je-sus and His
walk with me now and His

glad praises sing; And from Jesus
hap-py prais-es, prais-es sing;
hap-py prais-es sing,

nev-er roam,___ Come, walk with
Walk with Je-sus, come and
Come and walk with

Him to the gates of home
walk with Je-sus to the gates of home, that hap-py, hap-py,
Je-sus to the gates of home,

sweet home.
sweet, sweet hap-py, hap-py home, that hap-py, hap-py home.
sweet home, that hap-py, hap-py home.

Moses, Take Your Shoes Off

Conrad Cook / Conrad Cook

"Moses, take your shoes off, you're on Holy Ground.
Moses, take your shoes off, you're on Holy Ground."
The fire that He saw burning is in my soul right now.
"Moses, take your shoes off, you're on Holy Ground."

FINE ending: you're on Holy Ground."

1. God's people were in bondage
2. In this day in which we're livin'

© Copyright 1982 Land of the Sky Music. All rights reserved. Used by permission of Integrated Copyright Group, Inc.

Db7 Ab Ab° Ab
with no one to lead___ them out, So___ God___ called on Mos -
we're just wait - in' for___ our change, So un - til He comes to get___
Ab/C Bb Bb13 Bb9 Eb7 Db/Eb
___ es to___ turn their steps___ a - bout;___ He___
___ us, we should of His love___ pro - claim;___ To a
Ab Db7
called him up - on___ a moun - tain, When he turned,__ he looked___
dy - in' world__ go tell___ it– to be read - y when the trum -
Ab Db7
1.
a - round,___ He said,__ "Mos - es,___ take your shoes__ off,
pet sounds,___ So it will
Ab Eb7 Ab
2.
Ab7 Db
you're on Ho - ly Ground._ be all right___ if our shoes come off,

be-cause we're on Ho-ly Ground. Heard Him say, Do you know that He took a trip to

saved your soul? You're on Ho-ly Ground. Washed you clean and
Cal-va-ry. He saved my soul and

made you whole. You're on Ho-ly Ground. I've been to the riv-er, I've
set me free. He gave me a joy that I

been bap-tized, You're on Ho-ly Ground. My soul got hap-py, there's a
can't ex-plain, So, I'll keep on sing-ing in

1. rea-son why. You're on Ho-ly Ground. I
2. Je-sus' name. I heard Him say,

D.C. al FINE

Beyond The Gates

Rupert Cravens
Rupert Cravens

1. Be-yond the gates of life so fleet-ing, There is for us a bet-ter home; A place where peace shall reign for-ev-er, And sighs and tears shall nev-er come.
2. Be-yond the gates, be-yond all sor-row, Be-yond the cares of earth's vain store; We'll have new joy be-yond ex-pres-sion, Glad praise we'll sing on Heav-en's shore.
3. Be-yond the gates of all sad part-ings, Where grief and pain our hearts make sore; We'll meet a-gain our own dear loved ones, And see their wel-come smiles once more.
4. Be-yond the gates in Je-sus' like-ness, For-ev-er-more we shall live on; I want to meet you, Chris-tian broth-er, I'll look for you when morn shall dawn.

CHORUS

Be-yond the gates, be-yond the sun-set, New life im-mor-tal for us waits; We'll be at home on life's fair morn-ing, Be-yond the gates, be-yond the gates.

© Copyright 1949 (renewal 1977) James D. Vaughan Music Publisher/SESAC, a div. of Pathway Music, P.O. Box 2250, Cleveland, TN 37320 in Gospel Echoes. All rights reserved. Used by permission.

I Heard About A Stone

Arr. by Kevin Spencer

1. I heard a-bout a Stone that was hewed out of a moun-tain, Lord, I heard a-bout a Stone that came roll-ing down from Bab-y-lon; I heard a-bout a Stone that was hewed out of a moun-tain, Lord, and tore down the king-doms of this world, oh, Lord.
2. I'm search-ing for that Stone that was hewed out of a moun-tain, Lord, I'm search-ing for that Stone that came roll-ing down from Bab-y-lon; I'm search-ing for that Stone that was hewed out of a moun-tain, Lord, and tore down the king-doms of this world, oh, Lord.
3. Ole Dan-iel saw that Stone that was hewed out of a moun-tain, Lord, Ole Dan-iel saw that Stone that came roll-ing down from Bab-y-lon; Ole Dan-iel saw that Stone that was hewed out of a moun-tain, Lord, and tore down the king-doms of this world, oh, Lord.
4. My moth-er had that Stone that was hewed out of a moun-tain, Lord, My moth-er had that Stone that came roll-ing down from Bab-y-lon; My moth-er had that Stone that was hewed out of a moun-tain, Lord, and tore down the king-doms of this world, oh, Lord.
5. — You can have that Stone that was hewed out of a moun-tain, Lord, — You can have that Stone that came roll-ing down from Bab-y-lon; — You can have that Stone that was hewed out of a moun-tain, Lord, and tore down the king-doms of this world, oh, Lord.

Arr. © Copyright 1992 Kevin Spencer Publishing/BMI. All rights reserved. Used by permission.

Let's All Go Down To The River

Earl Montgomery
Sue Richards

Let's all go down to the riv-er, yes, there's a Man walk-in' on the wa-ter. Come a-long with me, all I want to see is this Man walk-in' on the wa-ter.

3rd time to CODA

1. He can raise the dead from the grave,   and change the wa-ter — and turn it in-to wine. He can make the
2. Je-sus is the Man at the riv-er, and He's wash-in' peo-ple's sin a-way. He can save your

© Copyright 1972 Music Corporation of America. All rights reserved. Used by permission.

lame walk. He can make the dumb talk, — — o - pen
soul. You give Him con - trol, and be read - y
up the eyes of the blind. So, wa - ter. To see the
for the Judg - ment Day. So,

D.C. al CODA ⊕ *CODA*

Sea Walk - er, the Blind Man Heal - er, that Lep - er Cleans - ing
Man from Gal - i - lee; To see the Soul Sav - er,
from Gal - i - lee;
the One who died for me. Take my hand and

36

Jesus Is All The World To Me

W. L. T.
Will L. Thompson

1. Je - sus is all the world to me, My life, my joy, my all;
2. Je - sus is all the world to me, My Friend in tri - als sore;
3. Je - sus is all the world to me, And true to Him I'll be;
4. Je - sus is all the world to me, I want no bet - ter friend;

He is my strength from day to day, With - out Him I would fall.
I go to Him for bless - ings, and He gives them o'er and o'er.
O how could I this Friend de - ny, When He's so true to me?
I trust Him now, I'll trust Him when life's fleet - ing days shall end.

When I am sad to Him I go, No oth - er one can cheer me so;
He sends the sun - shine and the rain, He sends the har - vest's gold - en grain;
Fol - low - ing Him I know I'm right, He watch - es o'er me day and night;
Beau - ti - ful life with such a Friend; Beau - ti - ful life that has no end;

When I am sad He makes me glad, He's my Friend.
Sun - shine and rain, har - vest of grain, He's my Friend.
Fol - low - ing Him by day and night, He's my Friend.
E - ter - nal life, e - ter - nal joy, He's my Friend.

I Don't Want To Live No More Without Jesus

C. H.

Carvel Horton

1. Man-y times I get dis-cour-aged won-d'ring what I can do,
2. Lone-ly roads I have to trav-el of-ten-times all a-lone,

Trou-bles seem to pile up on me with no an-swer in view;
Seems I have no earth-ly help, my friends and loved ones are gone;

Then a voice with-in me whis-pers there is One who still cares,
Great-er love is wait-ing for me at the end of this road,

On your knees and call on Je-sus, He will an-swer your prayer.
I've a place just wait-ing for me at the end of this road.

CHORUS

Live no more, live no more,
I don't want to live no more with-out
Live no more, live no more,
I don't want to live no more with-out

© Copyright 1982 Onward Bound Music. All rights reserved. Used by permission of Integrated Copyright Group, Inc.

In loving memory of Rosie Rozell,
August 29, 1928 - February 28, 1995

I Lost It All To Find Everything

William J. & Gloria Gaither
William J. Gaither

1. I had won all I could win, there was no place I hadn't been, But my heart was just so needy and so poor; Then I heard Him gently say, "Lose it all and find My way," so, I gave it up and I found it all and more. I lost it

© Copyright 1976 William J. Gaither. All rights reserved.

all to find ev-'ry-thing. I died a pauper to be-come a king. When I learned how to lose, I found how to win. Oh, I lost it all to find ev-'ry-thing.

FINE

2. I was fran-tic to sur-vive and I was rac-ing to a-rise and I walked on an-y stand-ing

The Statesmen Quartet

At The Cross

Isaac Watts
Refrain added by Ralph E. Hudson

Ralph E. Hudson

1. A-las and did my Sav-ior bleed? And did my Sov-'reign die?
   Would He de-vote that sa-cred head For some-one such as I?
2. Was it for crimes that I have done, He suf-fered on the tree?
   A-maz-ing pit-y! grace un-known! And love be-yond de-gree!
3. Well might the sun in dark-ness hide And shut His glo-ries in,
   When Christ, the might-y Mak-er, died For man, the crea-ture's sin.
4. But drops of grief can ne'er re-pay The debt of love I owe.
   Here, Lord, I give my-self a-way. 'Tis all that I can do!

REFRAIN

At the cross, at the cross where I first saw the light, And the bur-den of my heart rolled a-way; It was there by faith I re-ceived my sight, and now I am hap-py all the day!

I Don't Belong
(Sojourner's Song)

Gloria Gaither
Buddy Greene

1. It's not home where men sell their souls and the taste of power is sweet; Where wrong is right and neighbors fight, while the hungry are dyin' in the streets; Where kids are a-bused and women are used and the

2. Don't be-long but while I'm here I'll be livin' like I've nothin' to lose. And while I breathe I'll just believe my Lord is gonna see me through; I'll not be deceived by earth's make-believe I'll

3. I belong to a kingdom of peace where only love is the law. Where children lead and captives are freed, and God becomes a Baby on the straw; Where dead men live and rich men give their

© Copyright 1990 Gaither Music Company, Rufus Music, and Spiritquest Music. All rights reserved. Used by permission.

weak____ are crushed by the strong,___ Na-tions gone mad,___
close my ears to her si-ren-song By prais-in' His name—
king-doms__ to buy back a song; — Sin-ners like me,___

— Je-sus is sad___ and I don't__ be-long.__
— I'm not a-shamed__ and I don't__ be-long.__
be-come roy-al-ty___ and we'll all__ be-long.__

CHORUS

I don't be-long—___ and I'm go - ing some-day,___
Yes, I be-long,___ and I'm go - in' some-day,___

Back to my own na-tive land.___ I don't be-long___
Home to my own na-tive land.___ Where I be-long___

and it seems___ like I hear the sound of a "wel-
and it seems___ that I hear the sound of a "wel-

46

come home" band. I don't be-long, I'm a for-
come home" band. Yes, I'll be-long— no for-

eign-er here— sing-in' a so-journ-er's song.
eign-er there sing-in' a so-journ-er's song;

I've al-ways known this place ain't home, and I don't be-long.
I've al-ways known I'm go-ing home — where I be-long.

C. M. "Shorty" Bradford

When You Pray

A. M.
Audrey Mieir

At the close of the day when you kneel to pray, Will you re-mem-ber me? I need help ev-'ry-day, this is why I pray. Will you re-mem-ber me?

When you pray will you pray for me, For I need His love and His care; When you pray will you pray for me, Will you whis-per my name in your prayer?

When I pray I will pray for you, For you need His love and His care; When I pray I will pray for you, I will whis-per your name in my prayer.

© Copyright 1959 Manna Music, Inc. All rights Reserved. Used by permission.

The Longer I Serve Him

William J. Gaither   William J. Gaither

1. Since I start-ed for the King-dom, Since my life He con-trols, Since I gave my heart to Je-sus, The long-er I serve Him, the sweet-er He grows.

2. Ev-'ry need He is sup-ply-ing, Plen-teous grace He be-stows; Ev-'ry-day my way gets bright-er, The long-er I serve Him, the sweet-er He grows.

The long-er I serve Him the sweet-er He grows, The more that I love Him, more love He be-stows; Each day is like heav-en, my heart o-ver-flows, The long-er I serve Him the sweet-er He grows.

© Copyright 1965 William J. Gaither. All rights reserved.

Rehearsal

Getting ready

Vestal & Sue

Two friends

What a group

Lillie Knauls

Vestal & Howard

The Martins

Chonda Pierce

The Bishops

Ivan Parker

Greg Cook & the Florida Boys

Mary Tom & Rosie Rozell

Jessy Dixon

Jake "Doing His Thing"

Stan Whitmire

Janet

Dallas Holm

Cynthia "The Voice of My Beloved"

James & Jimmy Blackwood

Ed Enoch

Nancy Harmon

Written In Red

G.J.
Gordon Jensen

1. In letters of crimson God wrote His love on a hillside so long, long ago. For you and for me — Jesus died and Love's greatest story was told.
2. Down through the ages God wrote His love with the same hands that suffered and bled. Giving all He had to give a message so easily read.

CHORUS

"I love you! I love you!" that's what Calvary said. "I love you! I love you! I love you! written in red."

© Copyright 1984 Word Music (div. of Word, Inc.). All rights reserved. Used by permission.

Heaven's Joy Awaits

V. B. (Vep) Ellis   V. B. (Vep) Ellis

1. When we leave this low-land, We will cross the Jor-dan, Past this chil-ly tor-rent, tor-rent, Heav-en's joy a-waits.
2. Heav-en's breeze is blow-ing, Gent-ly to me call-ing, I will soon be go-ing, go-ing, Thru the pearl-y gates.

Past the blue ho-ri-zon is Heav-en, Past the star-ry sky,
Just be-yond the blue ho-ri-zon, Just a-bove the star-ry sky, star-ry blue sky,
Be-yond the ho-ri-zon, ho-ri-zon is Heav-en, Just o-ver the star-ry sky, sky a-bove us,
Just be-yond the az-ure blue Past the star-ry sky, sky a-bove,

© Copyright 1942 by V. B. (Vep) Ellis. All rights reserved. Used by permission.

E♭ Fm7/C Cm A♭
Far a - bove this sor - row, I'll go a -
Far a - bove this land of sor - row,
I'm leav - ing this land of, of sor - row, I'll go a -
Far a - bove this land of woe,
E♭ Cm B♭7 E♭ B♭7
way,
way, a - bove each tear and sigh, ev - er - y sigh
way, sigh for - got - ten,
way, tears are gone,
E♭ Fm7/C Cm A♭
Few more miles be - fore us, And there is
Just a few more miles be - fore us,
Not man - y more miles to be go - ing, And there is
Just a few more wea - ry miles,
E♭ F7 B♭
Just a while to wait,
Just a lit - tle while to wait, pa - tient - ly wait,
There's just a lit - tle while to wait, wait for Je - sus,
Just a while to wait, Then we will

52

Sing re-demp-tion's cho-rus, I'm going
Soon we'll sing re-demp-tion's cho-rus,
We will sing re-demp-tion's glad cho-rus, I'm going
sing re-demp-tion's cho-rus grand,

up there where Heav-en's joy a-waits.
Heav - en's joy a-waits, Heav-en a-waits.
up there where Heav-en's joy a-waits.
Heav - en's joy a-waits.

The Harmoneers....Charles Key, Bobby Strickland, Fred C. Maples, Bob Crews, "Low Note" Hilton

My Jesus, I Love Thee

William R. Featherstone
Adoniram J. Gordon

1. My Jesus, I love Thee, I know Thou art mine;
2. I love Thee because Thou hast first loved me,
3. I'll love Thee in life, I will love Thee in death,
4. In mansions of glory and endless delight,

For Thee all the follies of sin I resign;
And purchased my pardon on Calvary's tree;
And praise Thee as long as Thou lendest me breath;
I'll ever adore Thee in heaven so bright;

My gracious Redeemer, my Savior art Thou;
I love Thee for wearing the thorns on Thy brow;
And say when the death-dew lies cold on my brow;
I'll sing with the glittering crown on my brow;

If ever I loved Thee, my Jesus, 'tis now.
If ever I loved Thee, my Jesus, 'tis now.
If ever I loved Thee, my Jesus, 'tis now.
If ever I loved Thee, my Jesus, 'tis now.

I Just Steal Away And Pray

Albert E. Brumley   Albert E. Brumley

1. Ev-'ry time I do a deed I should not do,
2. Oft-en-times I'm made to bow my head in shame
3. Christ, the Sav-ior, al-ways hears and an-swers pray'r,

Ev-'ry time I say a word I should not say;
At some i-dle thought or deed a-long life's way;
And He gives me man-y bless-ings ev-'ry day;

Let me tell you what I do and it brings a bless-ing too,
But I nev-er am a-shamed of my Sav-ior's pre-cious name,
So when I have tried my best and I've failed to pass the test,

I just steal a-way some-where and pray.

© Copyright 1974 by Stamps Quartet Music.
All Rights Reserved. Used by permission of Integrated Copyright Group, Inc..

55

CHORUS

I just steal a-way, I just steal a-way,

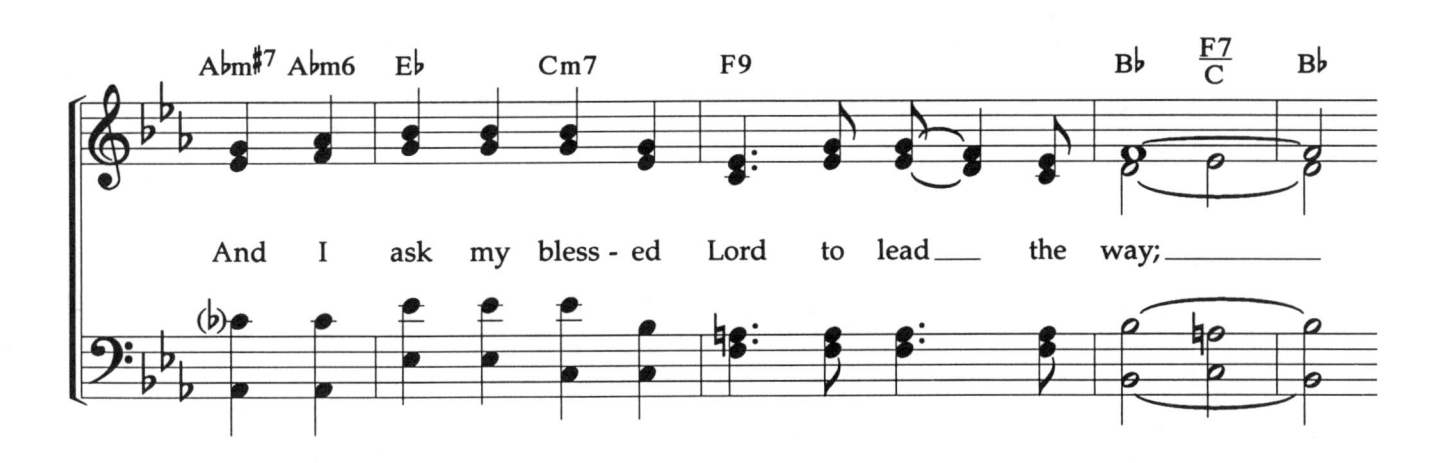

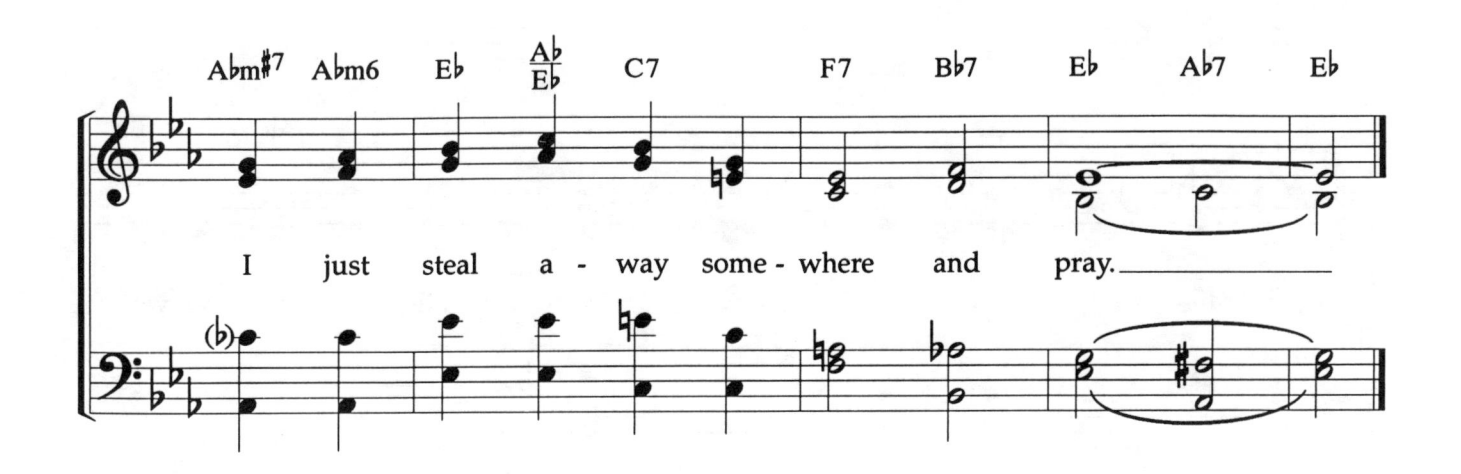

And I ask my bless-ed Lord to lead the way;

I just steal a-way, I just steal a-way,

I just steal a-way some-where and pray.

Life Will Be Sweeter Someday

Arranged by David Reese

Je-sus said, I be-lieve Him, Life will be sweet-er some-day. I'm gon-na trust Him, nev-er doubt Him, no mat-ter what the folks may say. Can't turn a-way from Him light-ly, be-cause the joys of Heav-en I'll miss, For I will live on up in Glo-ry af-ter while, af-ter while.

Don't you know I'm gon-na sing, / sing with the an-gels a-bove. I'm gon-na talk / talk to the ones that I love. I'm gon-na tell Him a-bout my trou-bles af-ter while, af-ter while. Oh well, I'm gon-na march / march down the streets of pure gold. I'm gon-na talk / talk to the proph-ets of old. I'll be hap-py up in Glo-ry af-ter while,

after while.__ Don't you know I'm gon-na sing, with the / sing / an-gels a-bove. I'm gon-na talk to the ones that I love. I'm gon-na / talk / tell__ Him a-bout my trou-bles af-ter while,__ af-ter while.__ Well,__ I'm gon-na march down the streets of pure gold. / march / I'm gon-na talk to the proph-ets of old. I'll__ be / talk hap - py up in Glo - ry af - ter while,____ while.

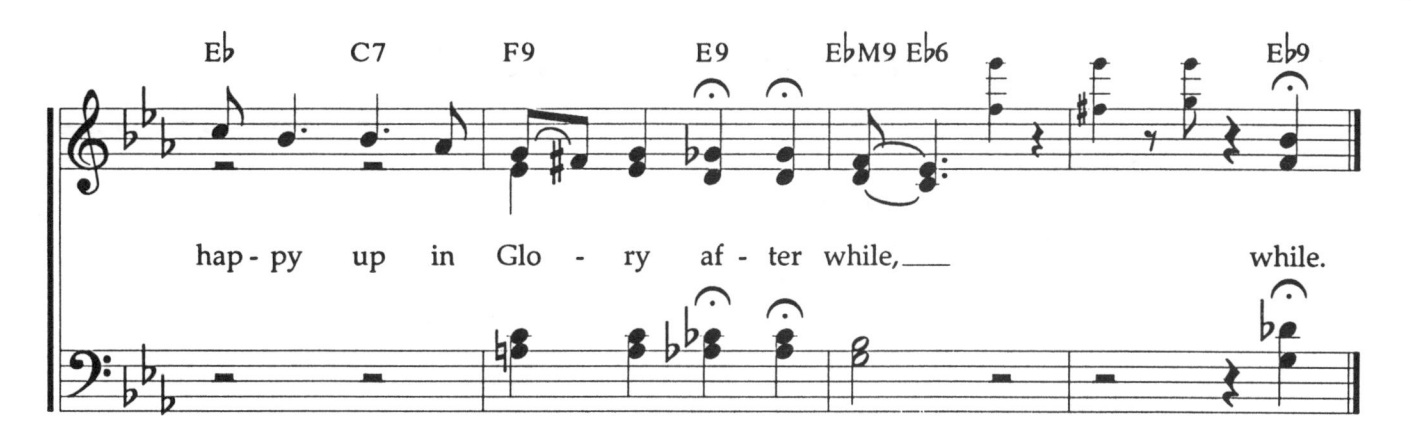

The Blackwood Brothers with Governor Jimmie Davis

Let's Have A Revival

J. H. & L. G.
Joel Hemphill & Lari Goss

CHORUS

Let's have a revival from the pulpit to the pew.

Let's have a revival that starts with me and you,

Then reaches out to a lost and hungry world to bring them in. This

is our joy, it's our survival. Let's pray for a

© Copyright 1987 Hemphill Music/Family and Friends Music (adm. by Benson Music Group, Inc.) and Lari Goss Music (adm. by Integrated Copyright Group, Inc.). All rights reserved. Used by permission.

Ho - ly Ghost ar - riv - al, let's have a re - viv - al.

1. Some - times we've just gone through the mo - tions, left the Spir - it out, No
2. I asked an old - time preach - er how re - viv - als came back there, He

pow - er in our pro - gram no vic - t'ry in our shout; But
said, "We al - ways start - ed down on our knees in prayer. Just

God will give us back the joy, let's o - pen up the Bi - ble,
o - pen up the two books: the song - book and the Bi - ble.

D.C. (3rd time al FINE)

lay a - side for - mal - i - ty, let's have a re - viv - al.
If you'll sing and preach the Word, you'll have a re - viv - al."

The Blood-Bought Church

Nancy L. Harmon
Nancy L. Harmon

1. They shall lift up their voice, they shall shout for joy.
2. O pick up your harp, O Zi-on of the Lord,
3. Let the earth be si-lent, O wind, cease to blow,

They shall cry a-loud and be free. They shall
Let the earth ring forth with His praise. All His
Ev-'ry cre-a-ted be-ing, fold your wings, For there's a

glo-ri-fy the name of the Lord,
chil-dren re-joice from the is-lands of the sea, It's the
new song be-ing sung with a new mel-o-dy,

Blood-Bought, the Church, the Re-deemed. And we are in the

ar-my of the Lord, We've been washed in the blood and we are go-ing

© Copyright 1986 Love Special Productions. All rights reserved. Used by permission.

forth; There is nothing that can stop this mighty moving force, With a shout of praise, a two-edged sword. Ev-'ry stronghold of bondage must fall beneath our feet, Ev-'ry pris-'ner held captive must be freed. For our deliverance has come through the power of the Son, It's the Blood-Bought, the Church, the Redeemed.

On Jordan's Stormy Banks

Samuel Stennett
Traditional

1. On Jordan's stormy banks I stand, and cast a wishful eye To Canaan's fair and happy land, where my possessions lie.
2. All o'er those wide extended plains shines one eternal day; There God the Son forever reigns and scatters night away.
3. No chilling winds nor poi-s'nous breath can reach that healthful shore; Sickness and sorrow, pain and death are felt and feared no more.
4. When shall I reach that happy place, and be forever blest? When shall I see my Father's face, and in His bosom rest?

CHORUS

I am bound for the promised land, I am bound for the promised land; O who will come and go with me? I am bound for the promised land.

Everybody's Gonna Have A Wonderful Time Up There

L. R. A.

Lee Roy Abernathy

ah____
1. — Listen, ev-'ry-bod-y, cause I'm talk-ing to you.___ —
2. — Lis-ten here, my sis-ter, we're not leav-ing you out.___ You
3. — When the trib-u-la-tions seem to dark-en the way,___ —
4. Now get your Ho-ly Bi-ble in the back of the book,___ the

ah_____ ah____
Je - sus is the on - ly one to car - ry you through.___ Now you
may not be a preach - er but you sing___ and shout.___ — —
that's the time to get down on your knees___ and pray.___ — —
book of Rev - e - la - tion, that's the place you must look;___ — —

ah____
bet - ter get you read - y for I'm tell - ing you why,___ —
What's the use to wor - ry if you've been___ re-deemed,___ 'cause
Ev - 'ry - bod - y gon - na have their trou - bles, too,___ —
If you un - der - stand it and you can if you try,___ —

ah_____ ah___ ah___
Je - sus is a com - ing from His throne on high;___ —
Heav - en's e - ven bet - ter than a mis - er dreamed;___ —
Got - ta be so care - ful 'bout the things we do;___ We're
Je - sus is a - com - in' from His throne on high;___ —

© Copyright 1947 Polygram International Publishing, Inc. All rights reserved. Used by permission.

Man-y are the wea-ry and the lone___ and sad,___ They're
Think a-bout the trou-ble you could save___ some soul,___
go-ing down the val-ley, go-ing one___ by one,___
Read-in' in the Bi-ble all the things that He said,___

gon - na wish they had-n't done the things___ they had,___
Tell them what to do to reach the shin - ing goal,___
Gon - na be re-ward-ed for the things___ we've done,___
Said He was a-com-in' back to raise___ the dead,___

How're you gon - na feel a-bout the things He'll say___
Sure - ly you can show them how to find the light,___
When we get to Heav-en and the prom-ised land,___
Are you gon - na be a-mong the cho-sen few,___

on that judg-ment day?
make the whole thing right. Oom pah, Oom pah,
then we'll un-der-stand. Ev-'ry-bod-y's gon-na have re-
will you make it through?

C
Oom pah, Oom pah, pah, Oom pah, Oom pah, Oom pah, Oom
li - gion in glo - ry, Ev - 'ry - bod - y's gon - na be sing - ing that
G
pah, pah, Oom pah, Oom pah, Oom pah, Oom pah, pah,
sto - ry, Ev - 'ry - bod - y's gon - na have a won - der - ful time up
D7
G
Oom pah, Oom pah, Oom pah, Oom pah, pah, Oom pah, Oom pah,
there, Oh, glo - ry hal - le - lu - jah! Broth - er, there's a reck - on - ing a
C
Oom pah, Oom pah, pah, Oom pah, Oom pah, Oom pah, Oom pah, pah,
com - ing in the morn - ing, Bet - ter get you read - y 'cause I'm giv - ing you the warn - ing,
G
D7
G
C/G
G
We'll Have a won - der - ful time up there.
Ev - 'ry - bod - y's gon - na have a won - der - ful time up there.

When I Meet You

V. B. (Vep) Ellis
V. B. (Vep) Ellis

1. Oh, when I meet you up in Heav-en, Up there where shin-ing crowns are giv-en, We'll talk to-geth-er, we'll walk to-geth-er hand in hand, hand in hand; We'll take a stroll be-side the
   When I meet you up in Heav-en, There where shin-ing crowns are giv-en, Talk to-geth-er, walk to-geth-er, hand in hand; Take a stroll be-

2. We'll nev-er know a dis-ap-point-ment, No-bod-y there will get de-spond-ent, There'll be no sad-ness, all will be glad-ness ev-er-more, ev-er-more; We'll join the saints of ev-'ry
   Nev-er know a dis-ap-point-ment, No one there will get de-spond-ent, Be no sad-ness, will be glad-ness, ev-er-more; Join the saints of

© Copyright 1953 by Chappell & Co. Copyright renewed. International Copyright Secured. All rights reserved. Used by permission.

69

time____ to spend to-geth-er, We'll nev-er
Have the time to spend up there.

have to hur-ry for there's lots of time; There'll be no

grief,____ There'll be no cry-ing, There'll be no
No more grief, there'll be no cry-ing,

pain,____ There'll be no dy-ing, O, when I
No more pain, There'll be no dy-ing,

meet you, Oh, when I greet you o-ver
When I meet you, When I greet you

The Blackwood Brothers with Jackie Marshall

No, Not One!

Johnson Oatman, Jr.   George C. Hugg

1. There's not a friend like the lowly Jesus, No, not one! No, not one! None else could heal all our soul's dis-eas-es,
2. No friend like Him is so high and ho-ly, No, not one! No, not one! And yet no friend is so meek and low-ly,
3. There's not an hour that He is not near us, No, not one! No, not one! No night so dark but His love can cheer us,
4. Did ev-er saint find this Friend for-sake him? No, not one! No, not one! Or sin-ner find that He would not take him?
5. Was e'er a gift like the Sav-ior giv-en? No, not one! No, not one! Will He re-fuse us a home in Heav-en?

CHORUS

No not one! No, not one! Je-sus knows all a-bout our strug-gles, He will guide 'til the day is done; There's not a friend like the low-ly Je-sus, No not one! No, not one!

We Shall See Jesus

D. W.
Dianne Wilkinson

We shall see Jesus just as He is.

1. Once on a hillside, people were gathered,
   Hoping to see Him as thousands were fed;
   He touched the blind eyes, healed broken spirits,
   moved with compassion He raised up the dead.

2. Once on a hillside, people were gathered,
   No-one showed mercy to the One who had healed them,

© Copyright 1981 by Homeward Bound Music. All rights reserved. Used by permission of Integrated Copyright Group, Inc.

Watch-ing as Je-sus was cru-ci-fied;
Yet Je-sus loved them as He suf-fered and died.

3. Once on a hill-side, people were gath-ered, For Jesus had risen and soon would as-cend;
Then, as He blessed them, He rose to the heav-ens And gave them His prom-ise to come back a-gain.

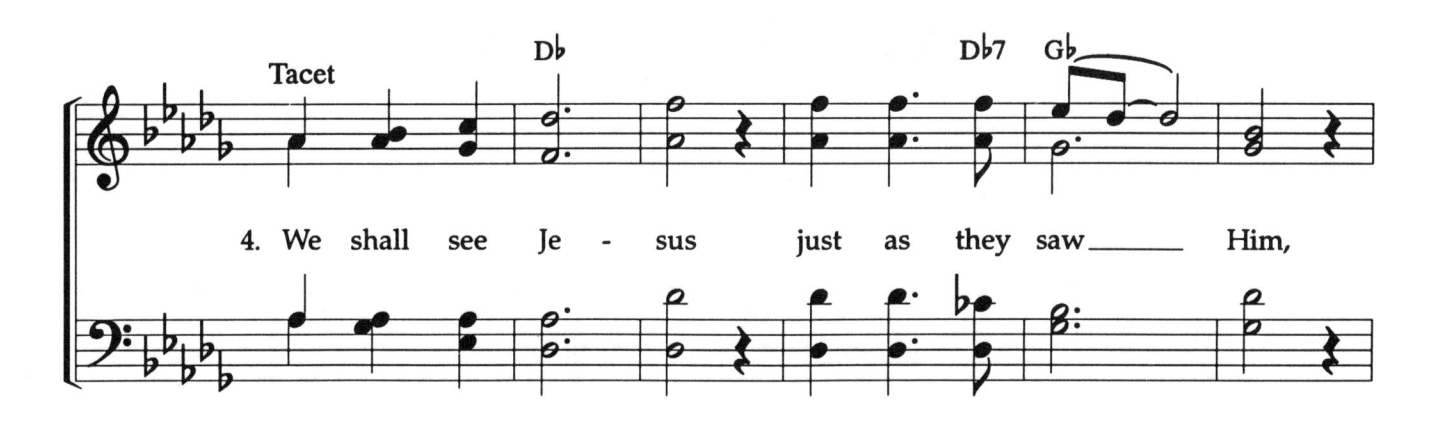

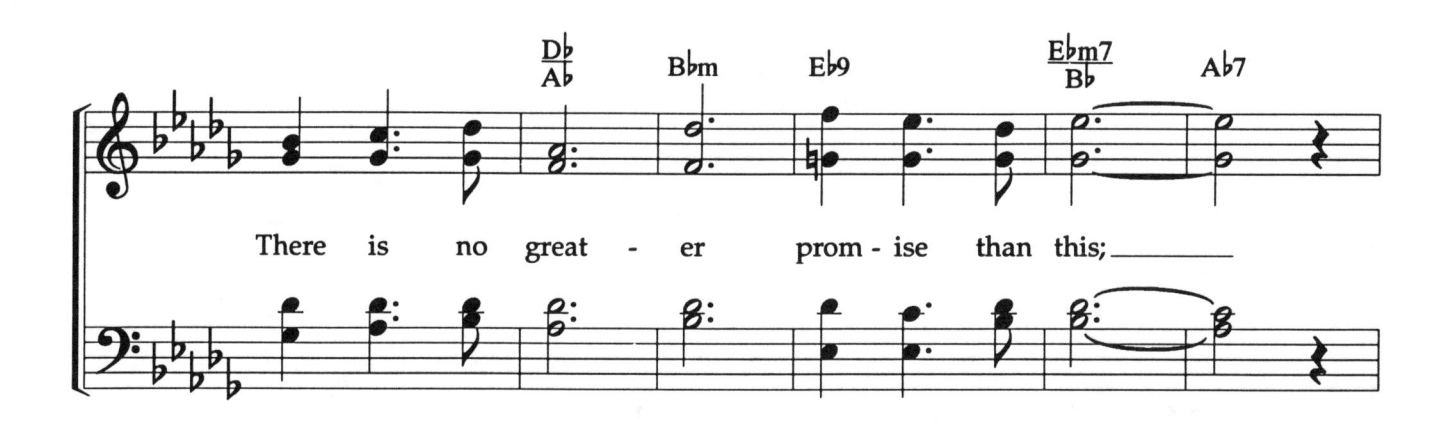

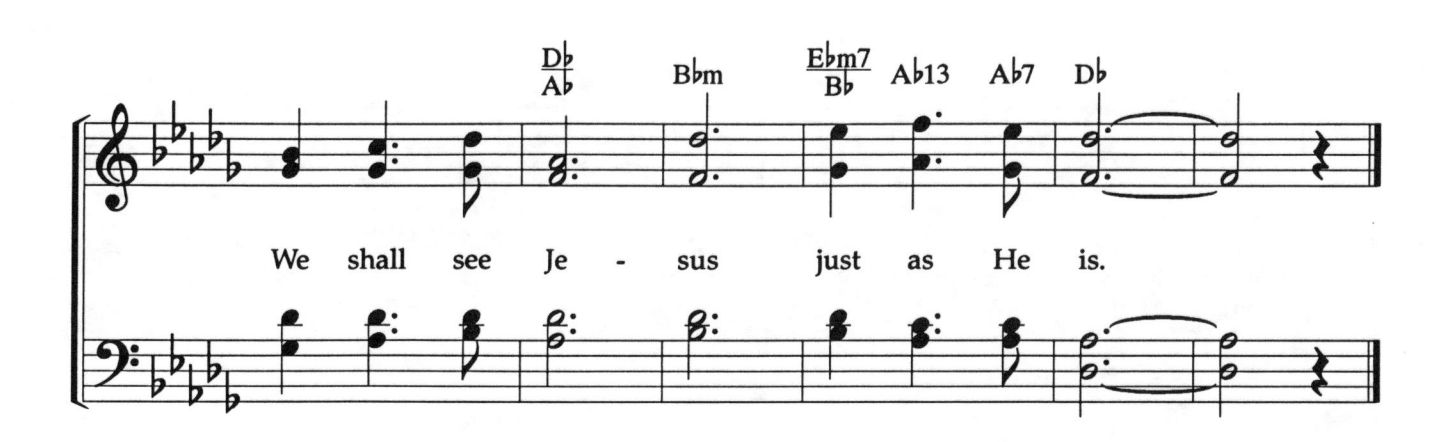

4. We shall see Jesus just as they saw Him,
There is no greater promise than this;
When He returns in power and glory,
We shall see Jesus just as He is.

Waiting For His Return

James B. Coats
James B. Coats

1. One day my soul was saved, saved from the fall, And then the Spirit came, came into my soul; Waiting for His return, His face to see, Go sailing through the air, I am waiting

One glad day my soul was saved, and then the Holy Spirit came to my soul, and now I'm waiting for the Lord's return, when I shall fly away to with Him ever be. I am waiting

2. O what a morn 'twill be, trumpets shall sound Calling the dead to rise, rise and brightly shine; From ev'ry sea and land they'll come with shouts, Changed so each one shall bear likeness that's divine. I am waiting

What a morning, when the trumpets sound to call the dead to rise up and shine, and from the sea and land they'll come with shouts, and they'll be changed to bear the

CHORUS

© Copyright 1949 by Stamps-Baxter Music. All rights reserved. Used by permission of Benson Music Group, Inc.

C7
F
G7/D C7/E
for Je-sus, to meet Him, and greet Him,
for the dear Lord, O how I yearn for His re-turn,
F
C7
Fire is burn-ing, 'tis burn-ing, Me in the
Fire is burn-ing deep in my soul, Keep-ing me in the Heav'n-ward
D.S. As I wait, I'll keep sing-ing, Love's news each
As I wait, I'll sing and be true, Tell-ing love's news each pass-ing
F F° F FINE
F7/A
B♭
A A♭
Heav'n-ward way. Night and day, all the way I have a song,
way. De-fends me, and sends me a song of gladness,
pass-ing day.
day.
G7
F F° F C7 D.S. al FINE
Al-ways near, He will cheer, guide me a-long;
He's near me, to cheer me, from sad-ness;

My God Is Real

K. M.
Kenneth Morris

1. There are some things I may not know, There are some places I can't go; But I am sure of this one thing That God is real for I can feel Him deep within.
2. Some folk may doubt, some folk may scorn, All can go on and leave me alone; I'll take God's part, And God is real for I can feel Him in my heart.
3. I cannot tell just how you felt When Jesus took your sins away; But since that day, yes, since that hour God has been real for I can feel His holy pow'r.

CHORUS

My God is real, real in my heart. Yes, my God is real,

© Copyright 1944 by Martin & Morris Music. Copyright renewed. All rights administered by Unichappell Music, Inc.
International copyright secured. All rights reserved. Used by permission.

Lee Roy Abernathy and Shorty Bradford

The Old Rugged Cross

G.B.
George Bennard

1. On a hill far a-way stood an old rug-ged cross, the em-blem of suf-f'ring and shame; And I love that old cross where the dear-est and best for a world of lost sin-ners was slain.
2. On that old rug-ged cross, so de-spised by the world, has a won-drous at-trac-tion for me; For the dear Lamb of God left His glo-ry a-bove to bear it to dark Cal-va-ry.
3. In the old rug-ged cross, stained with blood so di-vine, a won-drous beau-ty I see; For 'twas on that old cross Je-sus suf-fered and died to par-don and sanc-ti-fy me.
4. To the old rug-ged cross I will ev-er be true, its shame and re-proach glad-ly bear; Then He'll call me some day to my home far a-way, where His glo-ry for-ev-er I'll share.

CHORUS

So I'll cher-ish the old rug-ged cross, 'til my tro-phies at last I lay down; I will cling to the old rug-ged cross, and ex-change it some day for a crown.

Sheri Easter

Gordon Jensen

The Nelons

Ivan, Roger & Debra Talley

Friends

The Rambos

The Hoppers

Howard & Vestal with Doug

The Pfeifers

The Kevin Spencer Family

The Talleys

Hovie on piano

The Mullins

The McDuffs

Kirk Talley & Jake

Ann Downing, Mary Tom (Speer) Reid, Lily Weatherford, Vestal Goodman

Don DeGrate and Strong Tower

Brian Free & Assurance

Larry Ford & John Starnes

Dave Boyer

John Starnes & Debra Talley

Hazel Slaughter

Big John Hall

John Starnes, George Younce & Jake Hess

Room At The Cross For You

Ira F. Stanphill
Ira F. Stanphill

1. The cross up-on which Jesus died is a shelter in which we can hide; And its grace so free is suf-fi-cient for me, and deep is its foun-tain— as wide as the sea.
2. Tho' mil-lions have found Him a friend and have turned from the sins they have sinned, The Sav-ior still waits to o-pen the gates and wel-come a sin-ner be-fore it's too late.
3. The hand of my Sav-ior is strong, and the love of my Sav-ior is long; Through sun-shine or rain, through loss or in gain, the blood flows from Cal-v'ry to cleanse ev-'ry stain.

CHORUS

There's room at the cross for you. There's room at the cross for you. Tho' mil-lions have come, there's still room for one— Yes, there's room at the cross for you.

© Copyright 1946 and renewal © 1974 by Singspiration Music. All rights reserved. Used by permission of Benson Music Group, Inc.

Move That Mountain

J. T.
Joe Thomas

1. When trou-bles pile up high as a moun-tain in the sky, Don't just sit a-round feel-ing blue. There's no need to cry if in faith you will re-ly. Noth-ing is im-pos-si-ble for you.
2. When your luck be-gins to slide down the rug-ged moun-tain side, Now, don't let wor-ries crowd your mind with fear; Hold your head up high; In the ear-ly by and by, all your trou-bles soon will dis-ap-pear.
3. When life is cold and bleak as a snow-capped moun-tain peak, Now, don't give up your hopes in de-spair; Then you can find a way, please be-lieve in what I say— Your trou-bles all will van-ish in the air.

CHORUS

You can move that moun-tain! you can move that moun-tain!

© Copyright 1982 Angle Music. All rights reserved. Used by permission.

Don't wait 'til to-mor-row, start to-day. You can move that moun-tain! You can move that moun-tain! Wher-ev-er there's a will, there's a way. ev-er there's a will, there's a way.

Take Me In The Lifeboat

Take me in the life-boat, (yes) take me in the life-boat,
It will stand the rag-ing storm; Oh, take me in the life-boat, (yes) take me in the life-boat, It will bear my spir-it home. home.

verses

1. Come,___ broth-ers and sis-ters, let's don't fall a-sleep, We'll
2. As the boat___ goes sail-in' through life's storm-y tide,

pray night and day___ or we'll sink___ in the deep;___
Let Je-sus lead you, — — let Him be your Guide;___

Moth-ers and Fa-thers, keep___ cry-ing a-loud,___ cry-ing,
Then on Heav-en's por-tals you'll be safe ev-er-more,___ You'll be

"Won't___ You take us in the life - boat?"___
safe be-cause you board-ed the life - boat.___

D.S. al FINE

The Speer Family

The Bible Told Me So

1. There's a time to reap and a time to sow. Good seed planted ev'ry day will grow and grow. The Bible told me so. The Bible told me so. There's a time to laugh and a time to cry, a time to live and there's a time to die. I know, the Bible told me so when the evening lights are low. (Oh-oh) The Bible

2. There's a time to work and a time to play, Scatter flowers on the way where'er you go. Oh-oh Oh-oh This I know. There's a time to win and a time to lose, a time when ev'rybody gets the blues. Oh-oh

D.S. There's a time to reap and a time to sow, a time to pray

told me so. The Bi-ble told me so. This I know.
Oh - oh
told me so. (Oh - oh) The Bi-ble told me

Oh, the good Lord watch-es o-ver ev-'ry-one morn-ing, noon and night.

He made the moon and He made the sun so our fu-ture would be bright.

CODA
so. The Bi-ble told me so. The Bi-ble told me so.
This I know. This I know. so.

Paradise Island

Oakley Sharpe

1. Pic-ture Heav-en as a lone-ly isle, Some-where far a-way; Where there nev-er comes a sun-set, Time is just one long e-ter-nal day.
2. Though we all must play the game of life, No one ev-er wins; But when life on earth is o-ver, Then some-where e-ter-ni-ty be-gins.

CHORUS

How'd you like to spend e-ter-ni-ty on Par-a-dise Is-land? Live be-yond the star-ry sky, be-yond the sky?
E-ter-ni-ty on Par-a-dise Is-land? How'd you like to live for aye a-way be-yond the star-ry sky? Song-birds fill the air with

D.S. Won't you come a-long and

© Copyright 1950, renewed 1978 Stamps Quartet Music. All Rights Reserved. Used by permission of Integrated Copyright Group, Inc.

With mel-o-dy on Par-a-dise Is-land,
mel-o-dy on Par-a-dise Is-land,
Come, go with me to Par-a-dise Is-land?
go with me to Par-a-dise Is-land?

Care can't in this land on
Earth-ly care can-not an-noy, there's joy up in this land on
Find the joy a-wait-ing
Leave your earth-ly care be-hind and find the joy a-wait-ing

1. high;
2. high;
you.
you, a-wait-ing you.

Land of en-chant-ment where dreams come true, 'Tis al-ways spring-time, skies are al-ways blue;
skies are al-ways blue;

The Holy Hills Of Heaven Call Me

Dottie Rambo
Dottie Rambo

1. The ho-ly hills____ of Heav-en call me,____ to man-sions bright____ a-cross____ the sea;____ Where loved ones wait____ and crowns____ are giv-en;____ The____ hills of home____ keep call-ing me.

2. ____ I see loved____ ones o-ver yon-der,____ ____ Tears are gone____ and hearts____ are free;____ And from the throne____ my Sav-ior beck-ons,____ And the hills of home____ keep call-ing me.____

CHORUS

This house of flesh____ is but a pris-on,____ Bars____ of bone____ hold____ my soul;____ But the doors of

© Copyright 1968 John T. Benson Publishing Co. All rights reserved. Used by permission of Benson Music Group, Inc.

clay__ are gon-na burst__ wide o-pen,__ When the an-gels set__ my spir-it free;__ I'll take my flight__ like the might-y ea-gle,__ When the hills of home__ start call-ing me,__ When the hills of home__ start call-ing me. (call-ing me)__

Thread Of Hope

Marcia B. Henry

Marcia B. Henry

1. The woman needed healing of that dreaded disease, Her money brought physicians, but only Jesus could bring relief; And though her last thread of hope was worn down to a strand, her heart held on to faith, 'til she could touch Him with her hand. 'Cause when you're hanging by a thread

© Copyright 1989 Manna White Music. All rights reserved. Used by permission of Integrated Copyright Group, Inc.

still you can climb life's moun-tain, Though the cliffs are rough and jag-ged you can cope; If you should slip and reach rope's end you'll find the end of His gar-ment, So don't let go of the last thread of hope. hope.

2. Is that you hang-ing on-to a frayed and fra-gile faith? Are you

94

cling-ing to the rocks a-bove the can-yon of dis-may? Reach out for the life-line, it will nev-er break in two, Hold fast and don't lose heart,___ once a-gain God will pull you through.___

D.S. al FINE

Mr. & Mrs. Albert Brumley

Did You Ever Go Sailin'?

Albert E. Brumley / Albert E. Brumley

1. There's an old ram-shack-le shack where in dreams I wan-der back and listen to those Southern mel-o-dies; 'Twas the place where I was born on a bright Oc-to-ber morn, And it's nes-tled cab-in at the end of my riv-er of mem-o-ries.

2. There's a moth-er old and grey at the end of mem-'ry's way, I will meet her there to-night a-mong the trees; With a smile of wel-come she so sweet-ly beck-ons me To that cab-in at the end of my riv-er of mem-o-ries.

3. When the twi-light shad-ows fall man-y child-hood voic-es call, Call me back a-gain to days that used to be; And in an-swer to their pray'r I will soon be sail-in' there To that cab-in at the end of my riv-er of mem-o-ries.

CHORUS
Did you ev-er go sail-in' down the riv-er of mem-o-ries

© Copyright 1938 Stamps-Baxter Music. All rights reserved. Used by permission of Benson Music Group, Inc.

to a lit - tle log cab - in that is nes - tled a -
mong the syc - a - more trees; Where the sun - shine is cheer - y
and noth - ing in the world grows drear - y, That's my cab - in
at the end of my riv - er of mem - o - ries.

In The Garden

C. A. M.
C. Austin Miles

1. I come to the gar-den a-lone,___ while the dew is still on the ros - es; And the voice I hear, fall-ing on my ear, the Son of God dis-clos - es.
2. He speaks and the sound of His voice___ is so sweet the birds hush their sing - ing, And the mel - o - dy that He gave to me with-in my heart is ring - ing.
3. I'd stay in the gar-den with Him___ tho' the night a-round me be fall - ing, But He bids me go; through the voice of woe, His voice to me is call - ing.

And He walks with me, and He talks with me, and He tells me I am His own;___ And the joy we share as we tar-ry there, none oth-er has ev-er___ known.___

Over In The Gloryland

Lee Roy Abernathy

Lee Roy Abernathy

1. There's a true sto-ry all a-bout glo-ry and the glad an-gel band
2. When I get yon-der nev-er to wan-der I shall be sat-is-fied
3. Now that I've start-ed, nev-er down-heart-ed, Ev-er the path is bright

(Heav-en's an-gel band); Won-der if it's been told to you (if it's ev-er been
(I'll be sat-is-fied), With the glad home pre-pared for me (with a man-sion pre-
(It is ev-er bright), Glo-ri-fy God in all I do (yes, in ev-er-y-

told to you); If I could tell you, how it would thrill you, You could then
pared for me); Through the glad a-ges, shout-ing His prais-es, Hap-py for-
thing I do); Hap-py in know-ing, dai-ly I'm show-ing oth-ers the

un-der-stand (you could un-der-stand) Why the Lord built a place for
ev-er-more (there for-ev-er-more), Sing-ing His praise e-ter-nal
paths of right (to the paths of right), Tell-ing the world His love is

© Copyright 1945 (renewal 1972) Tennessee Music and Printing/ASCAP, a div of Pathway Music,
P. O. Box 2250, Cleveland, TN 37320 in <u>Songs Divine</u>. Used by permission.

CHORUS

you (a place for you).
ly (e - ter - nal - ly).
true (His love is true).

O - ver there 'tis al - ways spring,
O - ver there 'tis al - ways
O - ver there this I know 'tis al - ways
O - ver there 'tis al - ways

O - ver there the joy-bells ring, Ev - er-more my soul shall
spring o'er there the joy-bells ring, I shout and
spring, Ev - er-more my soul shall
spring, my soul will shout and

sing, with the an - gel band, I'm on - ly wait-ing for that hap - py day
sing, with the an - gel band, I'm on - ly wait-ing for that hap - py,
sing, I'm on - ly wait-ing for that glad day, that hap - py
sing, wait-ing for that hap - py

when my soul will sail a - way, O - ver in the Glo - ry land.
when my soul will sail and I reach Glo - ry - land.
day, O - ver in the Glo - ry - land.
day, and I reach Glo - ry - land.

He Bought My Soul At Calvary

S. H.
Stuart Hamblen

1. — There's a cross for ev-'ry-one to bear, but there's a Heav-en for each soul to share; — There's a place in Heav-en wait-ing me. I got it through His death at Cal-va-ry. Each drop of blood bought me a mil-lion years.

2. Tho' days are long and oft-en filled with care, I talk to Him and with each won-d'rous pray'r; He bids me stay and gives new strength to me. He bought my soul through death at Cal-va-ry. Each year that rolls I'm near-er to His side.

© Copyright 1950, renewed 1978 Hamblen Music Company. All rights reserved. Used by permission.

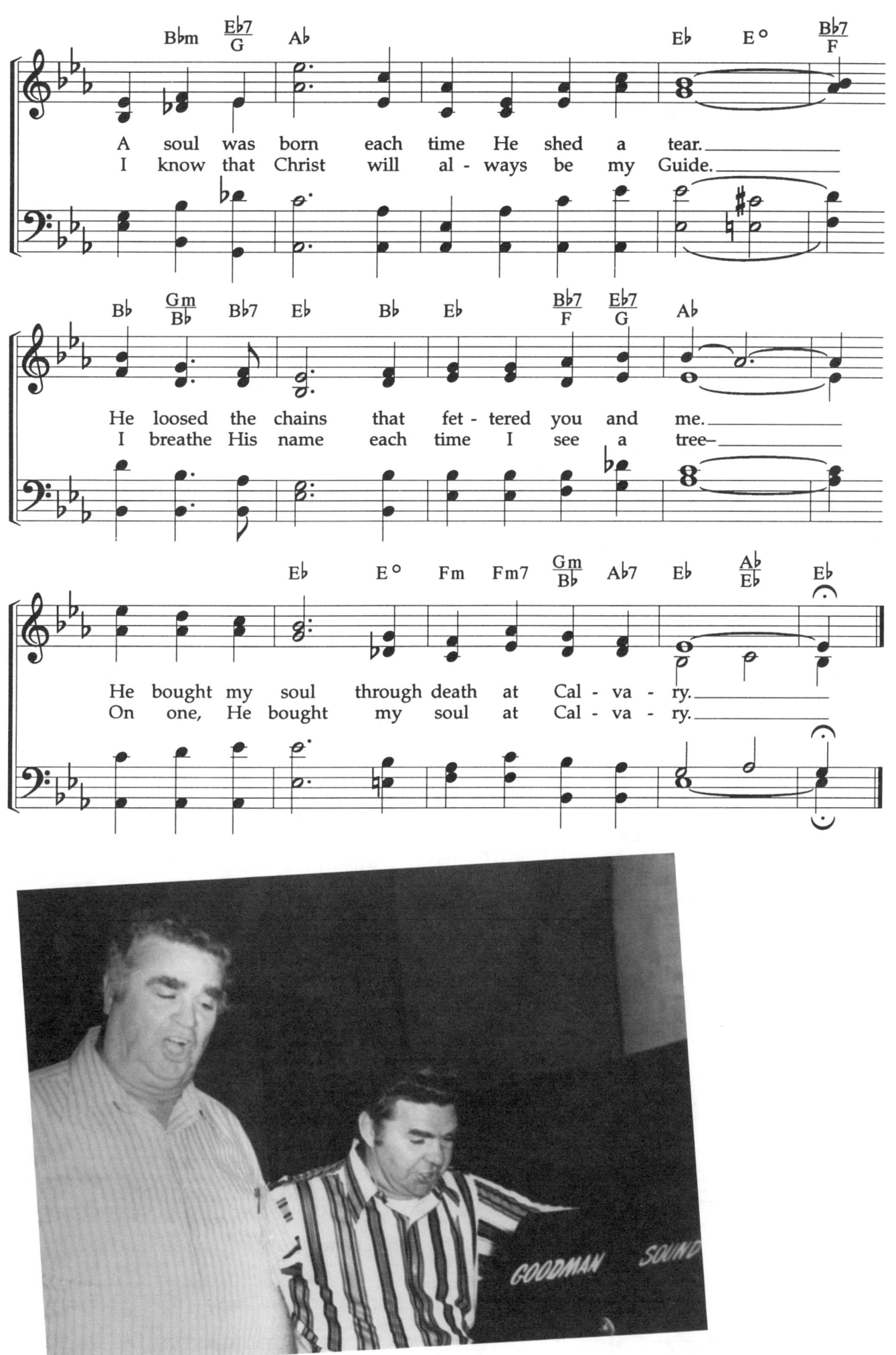

Howard and Sam Goodman

Sinner's Plea
(Male Quartet)

Joe Roper

Joe Roper

Through this world and its sin, I have wan-dered in need of a friend, (in need of a friend) I've been told of Your deeds, "Please, help me to-day" is my plea. (my humble plea)

CHORUS

Hear my cry, hear my call, Take my hand, Cleanse my soul, lift me up, help me stand;
Ah Lord, take my hand,
Ooh Yes, help me to stand;

© Copyright 1960, renewed 1988 by Faith Music. All rights reserved. Used by permission of Integrated Copyright Group, Inc.

I'm so blue, all a - lone, Please Lord, guide my
soul to Your home. (up to Your home) Hear my cry, hear my call,
Ah
Take my hand, Cleanse my soul, lift me up,
Lord, take my hand, Ooh
help me stand; I'm so blue, all a -
Yes, help me to stand;
lone, Please Lord, guide my soul to Your home, up to Your home.

I Believe In A Hill Called Mount Calvary

Dale Oldham, Gloria Gaither & William J. Gaither — William J. Gaither

1. There are things as we travel this earth's shifting sands that transcend all the reason of man; But the things that matter the most in this world, they can never be held in our hand.
2. I believe that the Christ who was slain on that cross has the power to change lives today; For He changed me completely, a new life is mine, That is why by the cross I will stay.
3. I believe that this life with its great mysteries surely someday will come to an end; But faith will conquer the darkness and death and will lead me at last to my Friend.

CHORUS

I believe in a hill called Mount Cal-v'ry — I'll believe whatever the cost; And when time has surrendered and

© Copyright 1968 by William J. Gaither. All rights reserved.

earth is no more, I'll still cling to that old rug-ged cross.

The Speer Family....Faye Speer, Ann Downing, Dad & Mom Speer, Brock Speer, Ben Speer, Charles Yates

We've Come This Far By Faith

Albert Goodson   *Albert Goodson*

We've come this far by faith, lean-ing on the Lord; Trust-ing in His ho-ly Word, He's nev-er failed us yet. Oh! We can't turn back, We've come this far by faith.

We've come this far by faith.

1. Don't be dis-cour-aged
2. Just re - mem - ber

© Copyright 1963 by Manna Music, Inc. All rights reserved. Used by permission.

with trou - ble ___ in your life; He'll bear your ___
the good things ___ He has done; Things that seemed im -

bur - dens and move ___ all ___ dis - cord and strife. Oh! We've
pos - si - ble, Oh, praise Him for the vic - t'ries He has won. Oh! We've

D.S. al FINE

A young Gordon Stoker

The Heavenly Parade

Adger M. Pace & J. T. Cook

Adger M. Pace & J. T. Cook

1. Our traveling days will soon be over here and we shall cross the rolling tide, For we are down here for just a little while, Our home is on the other side; Ambassadors true for Jesus, our Redeemer, and it is a love crusade For right against wrong, but soon we'll join the throng in Heaven when the saints parade.

2. Our stay upon earth cannot be very long for we are only passing through, A mission of love from Heaven up above to tell of our Redeemer true; He gave His own life in shame upon the tree, a ransom for the world He paid. So tell it in song, 'twill not be very long till we shall join the saint's parade.

3. So happy are we in telling you, my friend, that Jesus can redeem your soul From ev'ry known sin, and make you pure within, joy-billows o'er you then will roll; A happy new song you will begin to sing to Jesus, He the way hath made To glory-land fair, you'll have a mansion there and join us in the saint's parade.

© Copyright 1937 Adger M. Pace and J. T. Cook. Assigned to James D. Vaughan Music Publisher & Stamps Quartet Music Co.. Renewed 1965 by James D. Vaughan (div. of Pathway Press, P.O. Box 2250, Cleveland, TN 37320) and Stamps Quartet Music Co., (adm. by Integrated Copyright Group, Inc.)/SESAC. Used by permission.

CHORUS

For Heav-en's King we glad-ly sing, The sto-ry old, yet, ev-er new;
For Heav-en's King we will glad-ly sing the sto-ry, Sweet sto-ry old, and yet, 'tis ev-er new;
For Heav'n's King of glo-ry, we glad-ly will sing the sto-ry, Won-der-ful sto-ry, 'tis old, yet, 'tis ev-er new;
For Heav-en's own King, for Heav-en's ho-ly King, so glad-ly we will shout and sing, The bless-ed old sto-ry, sing it to His glo-ry, old, yet it is ev-er new;

In glo-ry-land with that
In glo-ry-land with that
In glo-ry up yon-der, with that
In glo-ry-land fair up yon-der in the air, with that e-

glad band, We'll prom-e-nade,
with that glad and hap-py band, Yes, we'll prom-e-
glad and hap-py band, We all then will

ter-nal, hap-py band, We'll prom-e-nade there and

nade_____ in Heav-en's pa - rade.
prom-e-nade in Heav'n in Heav-en's grand pa-rade.
in that grand pa-rade.

nev-er know a care, in Heav-en in a grand pa-rade.

The Dixie Four.... Gene Lowery, Melvin Doss, Shorty Green, Honey Dunn, Frankie Collins

Go, Tell It On The Mountains

John W. Work
American Folk Song

Go, tell it on the mountains, over the hills and ev-'ry-where; Go, tell it on the mountains that Jesus Christ is born.

1. 'Twas in a lowly manger that Jesus Christ was born; The Lord sent down a band of holy angels that bro't them a glorious morn.

2. Now, when I was a seeker, I sought both night and day; I asked the Lord if He could help me and He showed me the way.

There's Power In The Blood

L. E. J.
Lewis E. Jones

1. Would you be free from your burden of sin? There's pow'r in the blood, pow'r in the blood; Would you o'er evil a victory win? There's wonderful pow'r in the blood.
2. Would you be free from your passion and pride? There's pow'r in the blood, pow'r in the blood; Come for a cleansing to Calvary's tide— There's wonderful pow'r in the blood.
3. Would you be whiter, much whiter than snow? There's pow'r in the blood, pow'r in the blood; Sin stains are lost in its life-giving flow— There's wonderful pow'r in the blood.
4. Would you do service for Jesus, your King? There's pow'r in the blood, pow'r in the blood; Would you live daily His praises to sing? There's wonderful pow'r in the blood.

CHORUS

There is pow'r, pow'r, wonder-working pow'r In the blood of the Lamb; There is pow'r, pow'r, wonder-working pow'r In the precious blood of the Lamb.

A Time of Worship

Bill & his buddy - Hovie Lister

Chuck Millhuff

James Howard, Gloria Stanphill, Lily Weatherford

Conrad Cook & Group

Jack Toney "Beyond the Gates"

Babbie Mason

Holy Ground

Two Old Timers

Larry Ford & John Starnes

Sheri Easter & Baby "Morgan," Ed Hill and Rosie Rozell, Candy Hemphill, Rosa Nell (Speer) Powell

Two Old Road Warriors

Jake singing "Faith Unlocks the Door"

Having fun

Ben helping Rosie

Vestal & Mark

Les & Mark

The McDuff Brothers

Ann and Gloria

Rosie

Rosie and Dean singing "Oh, What a Savior"

Vestal singing "The Answer's on its Way"

Mark & Vestal huggin'

Wait Till You See Me In My New Home

Joe Parks
Joe Parks

1. Here on earth you may talk and brag about all your wealth un- told, A- bout your sil- ver and your gold; Man- sions on dis- play, homes in bright ar- ray, mock me as I roam, Just wait till you see my new home. Own a man- sion, If a man- sion you own while here on earth I now roam, just wait till you see me in my new home.

2. You may talk a- bout paint- ed walls and a- bout your mir- rors fair, A- bout your gar- den land- scapes rare; You may laugh at my plight each night as I sleep neath Heav- en's dome, Just wait till you see my new home. Cas - tle sport- ing, If a cas - tle you're sport- ing, dev - il court- ing, wait till you see while the dev - il you're court- ing, wait till you see me in my new

CHORUS

© Copyright 1949, (renewal 1977) by Tennessee Music & Printing/ASCAP, a div. of Pathway Music, P.O. Box 2250, Cleveland, TN 37320 in <u>Living Jewels</u>. Used by permission.

home. You talk a-bout
home. Broth-er, here on earth we talk a-bout
your price-less jew-els rich and rare. I praise the Lord
Ev-'ry-day I
praise the bless-ed Lord for man-sions bright be-yond com-pare, So,
think a won-der, goods you squan-der,
if you think you're a won-der, earth-ly goods you now squan-der,
wait till you see home.
wait till you see me in my new home.

Soon And Very Soon

Andraé Crouch / Andraé Crouch

1, 4. Soon and ver-y soon,___ we are going to see the King;___
2. No more cry-ing there,___ we are going to see the King;___
3. No more dy-ing there,___ we are going to see the King;___

Soon and ver-y soon,___ we are going to see the King;___
No more cry-ing there,___ we are going to see the King;___
No more dy-ing there,___ we are going to see the King;___

Soon and ver-y soon,___ we are going to see the King;___
No more cry-ing there,___ we are going to see the King;___
No more dy-ing there,___ we are going to see the King;___

Hal-le-lu-jah!___ Hal-le-lu-jah!___ We're going to see the King.___

going to see the King.___ Hal-le-lu-jah! Hal-le-lu-jah!

© Copyright 1976 Bud John Songs, Inc./Crouch Music. All rights controlled and administered by EMI Christian Music Publishing. Used by permission.

Sweeter As The Days Go By

Genser Smith   *Genser Smith*

1. The more I trust Him, the more I love Him, — Nothing good for me He'll deny; The longer I know Him, the better I can show Him, I couldn't stop now if I tried.
2. The moment He saved me, His good grace He gave me, He placed His love down deep in my heart; It's great joy in knowing with Him I am going, And nevermore from Him to depart.

CHORUS

Oh, it gets sweeter as the days go by, It gets sweeter as the moments

© Copyright 1961 LeFevre-Sing Publishing. All rights reserved. Used by permission of Integrated Copyright Group, Inc.

fly; His love is rich-er, deep-er, full-er, sweet-er, Sweet-er, sweet-er, sweet-er as the days go by.

Dad Speer

The Love Of God

V. B. (Vep) Ellis   V. B. (Vep) Ellis

1. The love of God has been extended to a fallen race; Through Christ, the Savior of all men, there's hope in saving grace. (saving grace.)
2. It goes beneath the deepest stain that sin could ever leave; Redeeming souls to live again, who will on Christ believe. (will believe.)
3. The flowers blooming in the spring, the heavens up above In silent declaration bring the story of God's love. (matchless love.)

CHORUS

Love of God greater far gold or silver ever could afford. Reaches past

The love of God is greater far than gold or silver ever could afford. It reaches past the wealth afford,

© Copyright 1949, renewed 1977 in Supreme Joy by Stamps Quartet Music.
All rights reserved. Used by permission of Integrated Copyright Group, Inc.

highest star covers, yes, it
highest star and covers all the
covers the

covers all the world; Power is eternal, e-
world; Its power is eternal,
world;

ternal, Its glory is supernal, supernal, When
Its glory is supernal, When

all this earth pass away,
all this earth shall pass away,

always be the love of God.
There'll always be the precious love of God.

I Want To Walk Just As Close As I Can

A. E. B.
Albert E. Brumley

1. For the truth and the right,__ pre-cious Lord, have I stood. Have these hands done as much__ as they real-ly could? Have these knees bowed__ down__ as__ oft as they should? I want to walk as close__ as I pos-si-bly can, (pos-si-bly can).__ Lord, I want to walk__ just as close__ as I can,__ And do my best__

2. Guide my feet, pre-cious Lord,__ when I'm tempt-ed and tried, In Thy shel-ter-ing fold__ let me safe-ly hide; For__ one lit-tle step__ is too far from Thy side,

© Copyright 1960, renewed 1988 by Albert E. Brumley & Sons. All rights reserved. Used by permission of Integrated Copyright Group, Inc.

Happy Edwards of the Harmoneers

He Ain't Never Done Me Nothin' But Good

D. R.

Dottie Rambo

CHORUS

Oh, well, He ain't nev-er done me noth-in',
He ain't nev-er done me noth-in',
done me noth-in' but good, noth-in' but good.
done me noth-in' but good.

4th time FINE

1. — Job was a right-eous man the Dev-il could-n't
2. — His-t'ry tells of Pol-y-carp, a mor-tal for the gos-pel
3. I gave my heart to Je-sus and I took Him as my

doubt it, He sure-ly loved His Sav-ior, there was
sake — They built a fire a-round his feet then
Sav-ior, — Cast my lot with a cho-sen few, then I

© Copyright 1968 by John T. Benson Publishing Company.
All rights reserved. Used by permission of Benson Music Group, Inc.

no doubt__ a - bout it, — — Sa - tan cursed His bod - y from his
tied him to a stake — but the fire would not con - sume him, so they
start - ed out t'ward Heav - en, — — Soon I was for - sak - en — my

feet to__ his head, then__ told him all his__
pierced him with a sword, — — Blood ran down, put__
friends left one by one, But the good Lord walked right a -

chil - dren — and his cat - tle__ were dead; Then__ Job's — —
out the fire, but__ still he__ praised the Lord, — — All__ these
long be - side me, He nev - er left me a - lone, Oh, He fed me when

Bb7   F
wife — said, "Why don't you__ curse__ your God and__ die," but
years I've served Him__ and He's al - ways done me__ good. I
I was hun - gry__ and He cheered me when I was__ sad. Oh,

D.S. (4th time al FINE)
Bb7   F
Job — said, — — "Wom - an,__ — you speak like a fool - ish child."
won't re - pent and I won't re - cant, just tell me__ why I should!
He has been the__ dear - est Friend this poor girl's__ ev - er had.

Saved By The Hands

Gloria Gaither & Terry & Barbi Franklin

Terry & Barbi Franklin

1. Hands that mul-ti-plied the bread when the hun-gry crowd was fed, Kind hands that heal, made tor-ment-ed spir-its yield; But I'd have nev-er be-lieved, when I was lost, those hands would find me, and I'd be saved by the hands of Je-sus. Saved by the hands

2. Cal-loused hands, scarred with nails, pulled me up when I fell, Hands that tore and hands that bled raised my soul from the dead; Hands they could not bear to see, Lord, they are so beau-ti-ful to me! I've been saved by the hands

CHORUS

© Copyright 1994 Gaither Music Company and Tylis Music.
Administered by Gaither Copyright Management. Used by permission.

F C A7
two gen - tle hands surround - ing my soul, When my
D7 G C G
world fell a - part His fin - ger-prints of de - liv - er -
G7 C C9/E F
ance all o - ver my heart, I've been saved by the
1. C G7 C
hands of Je - sus.
2. C A7 D7 C/E
hands – two gen - tle hands,
F C G7 F C
Saved by the hands of Je - sus.

I'm Bound For That City

Albert E. Brumley, Bill Brumley, Robert Brumley, & Albert E. Brumley, Jr.

1. There's a City of light where there cometh no night, For the sun never sets in the sky; In the Bible we're told that the streets are pure gold, and a cool gentle river runs by.

2. Little children will play and our hearts will be gay, As we stroll through the City of gold; No more dying up there, no more sorrow to bear, and nobody will be feeble and old.

CHORUS

I'm bound for that City, God's holy white City, O yes, I am. I'll never turn back

© Copyright 1954, renewed 1982 by Albert E. Brumley & Sons.
All rights reserved. Used by permission of Integrated Copyright Group, Inc.

Two great basses – Big Jim Waite and Arnold Hyles. Hovie Lister on the piano

When I Make My Last Move

H. B.
Herbert Buffum

1. I've been trav-'ling for Je-sus so much of my life, I've been trav-'ling on land and on sea; But I'm count-ing on tak-ing a trip to the sky, That will be the last move for me.
2. I've seen won-der-ful sights as I've trav-eled a-far, But how lit-tle, how emp-ty 'twill seem; When I make my last move to that Cit-y of gold, And be-hold what no vi-sion could dream.
3. There'll be proph-ets of yore, whom I'll meet o-ver there, And whose teach-ings have guid-ed me right; I shall meet the a-pos-tles and Je-sus, my Lord, I be-lieve I shall know them at sight.
4. Here I'm both-ered with pack-ing each time that I move, And I car-ry a load in each hand; But I'll not need one thing I have used in this world, When I move to that Heav-en-ly Land.

CHORUS

When I move to the sky, up to Heav-en on high, What a won-der-ful trip that will be! I'm all read-y to go, washed in Cal-va-ry's flow; That will be the last move for me.

© Copyright 1926 by Mrs. John A. Anderson. International copyright 1939 by R. E. Winsett Co. All rights reserved. Used by permission.

Peace, Peace, Wonderful Peace

W. D. Cornell
W. G. Cooper

1. Far a-way in the depths of my spir-it to-night rolls a mel-o-dy sweet-er than psalm; In ce-les-tial-like strains it un-ceas-ing-ly falls o'er my soul like an in-fi-nite calm.
2. What a treas-ure I have in this won-der-ful peace, bur-ied deep in the heart of my soul; So se-cure that no pow-er can mine it a-way, while the years of e-ter-ni-ty roll.
3. I am rest-ing to-night in this won-der-ful peace, rest-ing sweet-ly in Je-sus' con-trol; For I'm kept from all dan-ger by night and by day, and His glo-ry is flood-ing my soul.
4. And me thinks when I rise to that Cit-y of peace, where the Au-thor of peace I shall see, That one strain of the song which the ran-somed will sing, in that heav-en-ly king-dom shall be.
5. Ah! soul, are you here with-out com-fort or rest, march-ing down the rough path-way of time? Make Je-sus your friend ere the shad-ows grow dark; Oh, ac-cept this sweet peace so sub-lime.

CHORUS

Peace! Peace! Won-der-ful peace, com-ing down from the Fa-ther a-bove; Sweep o-ver my spir-it for-ev-er I pray, in fath-om-less bil-lows of love.

He'll Find A Way

Donna Douglas / Donna Douglas

1. At times the load is heavy, at times the road is long, When circumstances come my way and you think you can't go on; When you're feeling at your weakest Jesus will be strong; He'll provide an answer when you've found all hope is gone, He'll find a way.

2. And at times your heart is breaking with a pain that's so intense, And all you hold is broken pieces to a life that makes no sense; He wants to lift you up and hold you and mend each torn event; He'll pick up the pieces that you tho't had all been spent,

For I know that if He can paint a

© Copyright 1987 C. A. Music (div. of Christian Artists Corp.) Administered by Music Services. All rights reserved. Used by permission.

Dm7/G G7 Cmaj7 Am/C Em/B Am7
sun - set and put the stars in place, I know if He can raise
Bm7 Em Am7 Am/D
up moun - tains and calm the storm - tossed waves; And if
Dm7 Dm7/G G7 Cmaj7 Cm7
He can con-quer death for - ev - er to o - pen Heav - en's gates,
Bm7 G/B Bm Em7 Am Am7/D
Then I know for you, I know for you, He'll find a way.
1. D.C.
Gsus G
2. D.S. al FINE
Gsus G
way! For I know that if
3.
F9sus F9 Cm G FINE
way! He'll find a way!

Rise Again

Dallas Holm

1. Go a-head, drive the nails in My hands; Laugh at Me where you stand;
Go a-head, and say it isn't Me; The day will come when you will see!

1. 'Cause I'll rise a-gain. There's no pow'r on earth can tie Me down! Yes I'll rise a-gain.
(2. 'Cause I'll) rise a-gain. There's no pow'r on earth can tie Me down! Yes, I'll rise a-gain.
(3. 'Cause I'll) come a-gain. There's no pow'r on earth can keep Me back! Yes, I'll come a-gain.

Death can't keep Me in the ground!
Death can't keep Me in the ground!
Come to take My peo-ple back!

© Copyright 1977 Going Holm Music and Dimension Music.
All rights reserved. Used by permission of Benson Music Group, Inc.

2. Go ahead and mock My name. My love for you is still the same; Go ahead and bury Me, But very soon I will be free! 'Cause I'll

3. Go ahead and say I'm dead and gone, But you will see that you were wrong; Go ahead and try to hide the Son, But all will see that I'm the One! 'Cause I'll

D.S. al FINE

Tennessee Ernie Ford with Hovie

Welcome Home, My Child

D. B.
David Beatty

1. I have traveled oh, so long with no place to call my home,
And I wondered if I'd ever find the way, find the way;
But I'm longing for the day when I hear my Father say,
"Welcome home, my child, from all your toil and care, toil and care."

2. When at last I end this life with the trouble and its strife,
And my friends are gathered 'round to say goodbye, say goodbye;
Now don't weep and cry for me, soon my Jesus I will see,
And I'll hear Him say, "My child, you're welcome home, welcome home."

© Copyright 1964 (renewed) Silverline Music, Inc. Administered by Warner Tamerlane Publishing Corp. All rights reserved. Used by permission.

Bb7 Bb° Bb7
"Wel- come home, my child," my Lord will
"Wel - come home, my child,"
Eb Bb7 Bb° Bb7
say, Wel- come home, my child,"
yes, my Lord will say, "Wel - come home, my child,"
Eb
one e - ter - nal day; I'll praise His
one e - ter - nal day; I'll praise His name
Eb7/G Ab
name through e - ter - ni - ty, When He says to
through e - ter - ni - ty,
Eb Bbm6/Db C7 F7 Bb7 Eb Ab/Eb Eb
me, oh, "My child, wel- come home."
When the Lord will say to me, "Wel- come home."

Stand Up For What I Stand For

Michael Sykes, Tanya Goodman Sykes, Mark Lowry, Norman Holland, George Hairr & Michael English

Michael Sykes, Tanya Goodman Sykes, Mark Lowry, Norman Holland, George Hairr & Michael English

1. The world has gone cra-zy, fol-low-ing things that aren't real, But the road that I've cho-sen is the high-way of life, The one that leads from Cal-va-ry to e-ter-ni-ty with Christ.

2. The three He-brew chil-dren cast in the fire long a-go, But they would-n't bow down, would-n't give in when the fire had died down, God was stand-ing with them! —

I'm gon-na stand up for what I stand for, Fight till the fin-ish and win the war;

© Copyright 1994 BMM Music (adm. by Gaither Copyright Management), Ariose Music (controlled and administered by EMI Christian Music Publishing), and Dayspring Music (div. of Word, Inc.). All rights reserved. Used by permission.

I'm gon-na keep on re-ceiv-in' from the One I'm be-liev-in';

I'm gon-na stand up for what I stand for!

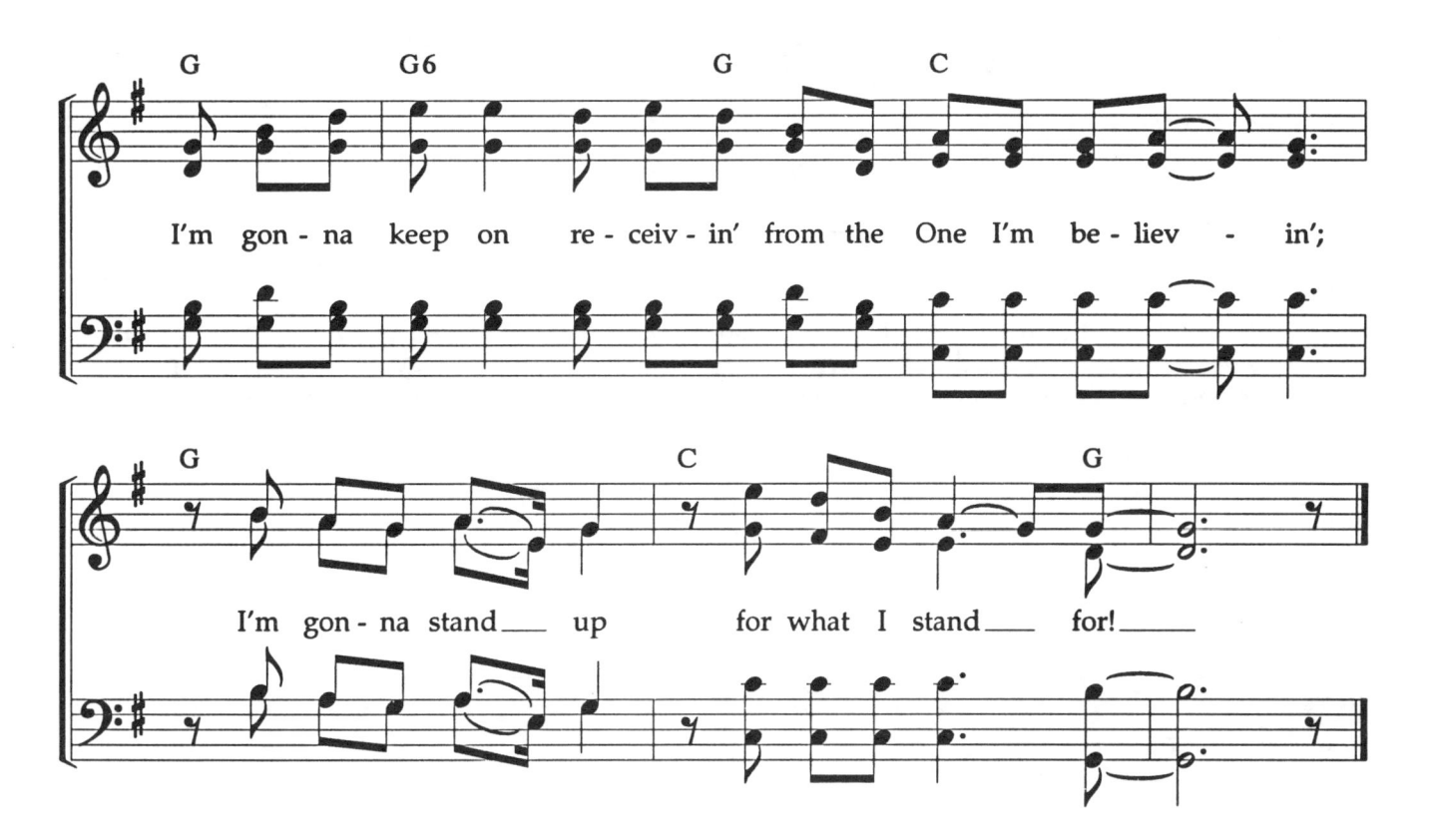

Bob Webber and Wally Fowler of the Oak Ridge Quartet

Won't It Be Glory There?

Lee Roy Abernathy
Lee Roy Abernathy

1. I have heard a-bout, I have read a-bout lands far o-ver the sea; And a hap-py place, where the saved by grace Shall for-ev-er be free. Get home, to roam, Glo-ry there?
2. I'm not wor-ried here when my path is drear, Joy is wait-ing I know; If I trust the Lord, I'll reap my re-ward, Where the faith-ful all go. When I get home, nev-er to roam, Won't it be glo-ry there?
3. When I reach that land on the gold-en strand, Oh, how hap-py I'll be; Sing-ing heav-en's praise through un-num-bered days, 'Twill be glo-ry for me. O-ver home, ne'er to roam, Oh, what glo-ry there.

CHORUS
When I get home,

© Copyright 1944 (renewal 1971) by Tennessee Music and Printing/ASCAP, a div. of Pathway Music,
P. O. Box 2250, Cleveland, TN 37320 in Songs Forever. Used by permission.

139

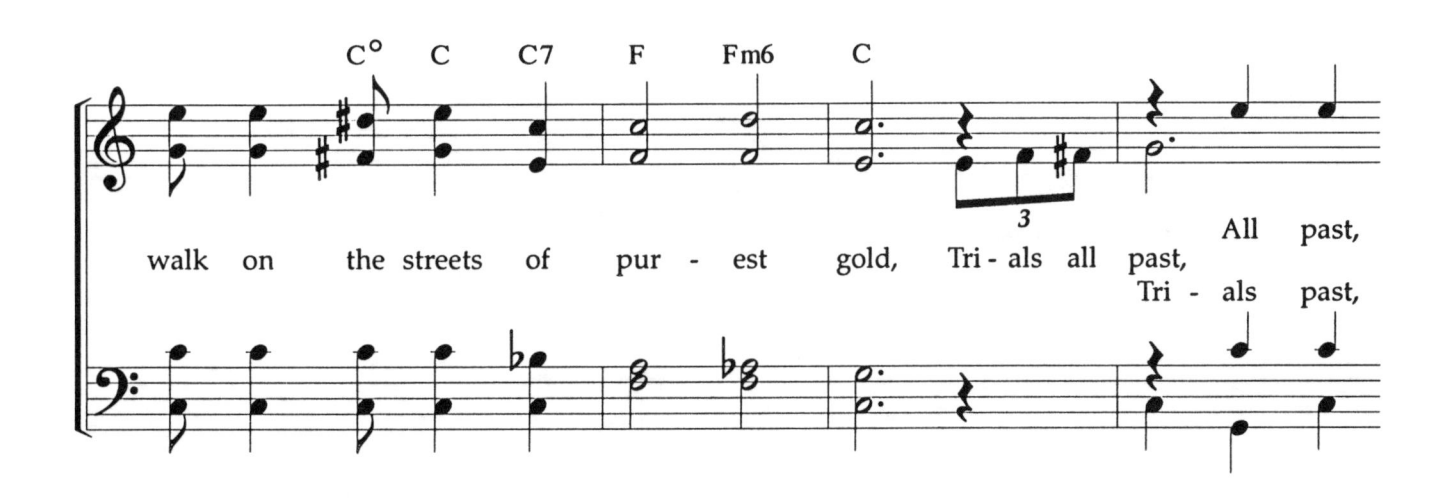

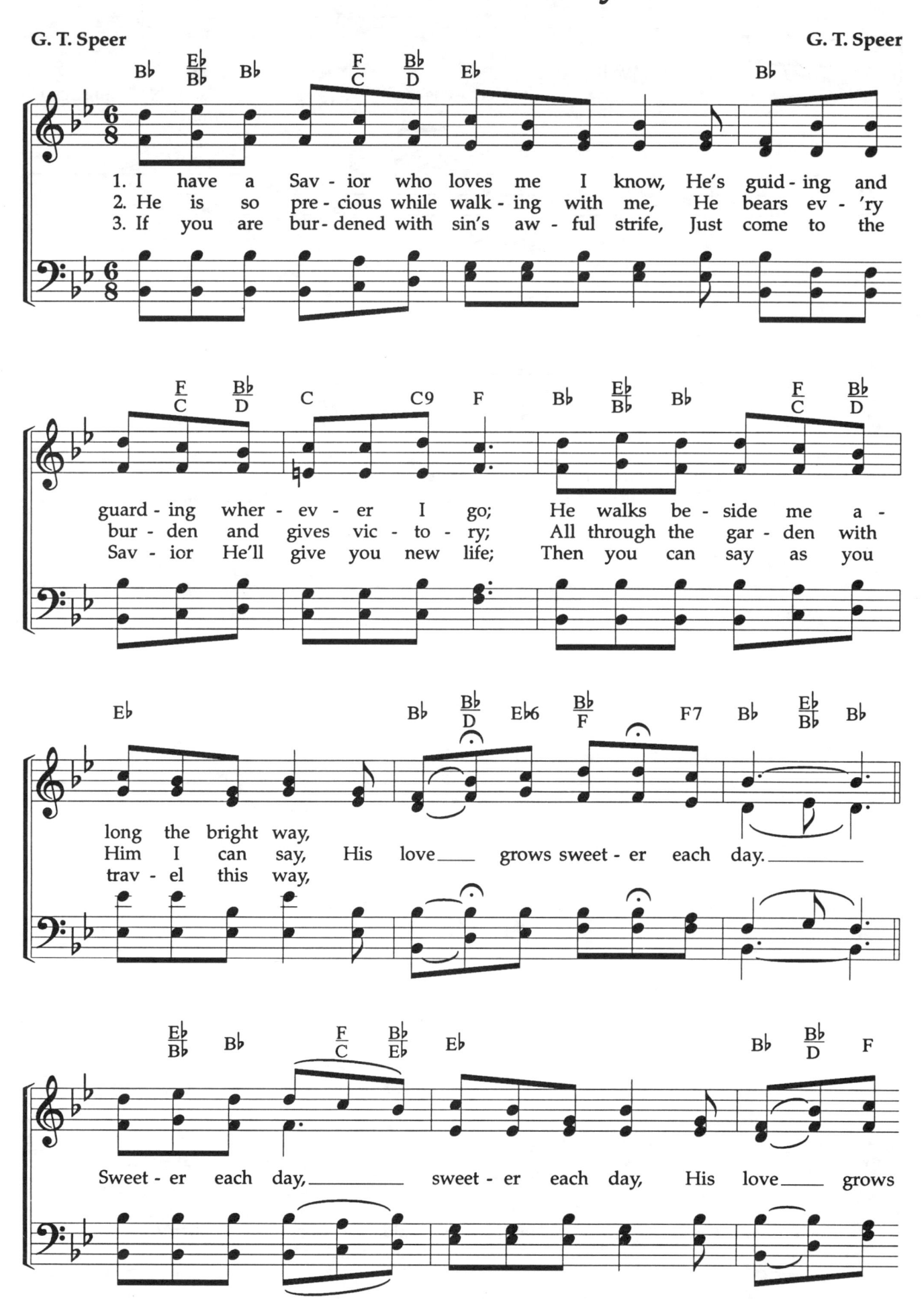

Sweeter Each Day

G. T. Speer
G. T. Speer

1. I have a Savior who loves me I know, He's guiding and guarding wherever I go; He walks beside me along the bright way, Him I can say, His love grows sweeter each day.
2. He is so precious while walking with me, He bears ev'ry burden and gives victory; All through the garden with Him I can say, His love grows sweeter each day.
3. If you are burdened with sin's awful strife, Just come to the Savior He'll give you new life; Then you can say as you travel this way, His love grows sweeter each day.

Sweeter each day, sweeter each day, His love grows

© Copyright 1946 Stamps-Baxter Music. All rights reserved. Used by permission of Benson Music Group, Inc.

sweet-er a - long the bright way; Sweet-er each day, sweet-er each day, His love grows sweet-er each day.

The Big Chief

Follow Me

Ira F. Stanphill
Ira F. Stanphill

1. I traveled down a lonely road and no one seemed to care. The burden on my weary back had bowed me to despair. I oft complained to Jesus How folks were treating me, And then I heard Him say so tenderly. "My feet were also weary, upon the Cal-v'ry road. The cross became so heavy,

2. "I work so hard for Jesus," I often boast and say, "I've sacrificed a lot of things to walk the narrow way. I gave up fame and fortune; I'm worth a lot to Thee." And then I hear Him gently say to me. "I left the throne of glory and counted it but loss. My hands were nailed in anger

3. O Jesus, if I die upon a foreign field some day, 'Twould be no more than love demands, no less could I repay. "No greater love hath mortal man Than for a friend to die." These are the words He gently spoke to me. "If just a cup of water I place within your hand, Then just a cup of water

© Copyright 1953 Singspiration Music. All rights reserved. Used by permission of Benson Music Group, Inc.

I fell be-neath the load. Be faith-ful wea-ry pil-grim the
up - on a cru - el cross. But now we'll make the jour-ney with
is all that I de-mand." But if by death to liv-ing they

morn-ing I can see. Just lift your cross and fol-low close to Me."
your hand safe in mine. So lift your cross and fol-low close to Me."
can Thy glo-ry see, I'll take my cross and fol-low close to Thee.

Bill Lyles

Shall We Gather At The River

R. L.
Robert Lowry

1. Shall we gath-er at the riv-er, where bright an-gel feet have trod;
2. On the bos-om of the riv-er, where the Sav-ior King we own,
3. Ere we reach the shin-ing riv-er, lay we ev-'ry bur-den down;
4. Soon we'll reach the shin-ing riv-er. Soon our pil-grim-age will cease.

With its crys-tal tide for-ev-er flow-ing by the throne of God?
We shall meet and sor-row nev-er 'neath the glo-ry of the throne.
Grace our spir-its will de-liv-er, and pro-vide a robe and crown.
Soon our hap-py hearts will quiv-er with the mel-o-dy of peace.

CHORUS

Yes, we'll gath-er at the riv-er, the beau-ti-ful, the beau-ti-ful riv-er,
Gath-er with the saints at the riv-er, that flows by the throne of God.

What A Lovely Name

Charles B. Wycuff

1. There's a name a-bove all oth-ers, Won-der-ful to hear, bring-ing hope and cheer; It's the love-ly name of Je-sus, ev-er-more the same, what a love-ly name.
2. Through His name there's won-drous pow-er, Pow-er to re-deem, mak-ing sin-ners clean; By His pow'r He cleansed the lep-er, o-pened blind-ed eyes, caused the dead to rise.
3. He'll re-turn in clouds of glo-ry, Saints of ev-'ry race shall be-hold His face; With Him en-ter Heav-en's cit-y, ev-er to ac-claim what a love-ly name.

CHORUS

What a love-ly name this name of Je-sus, reach-ing high-er

© Copyright 1967 Tennesse Music and Printing, a div. of Pathway Music, P.O. Box 2250 Cleveland, TN 37320 in Voice of Love. Used by permission.

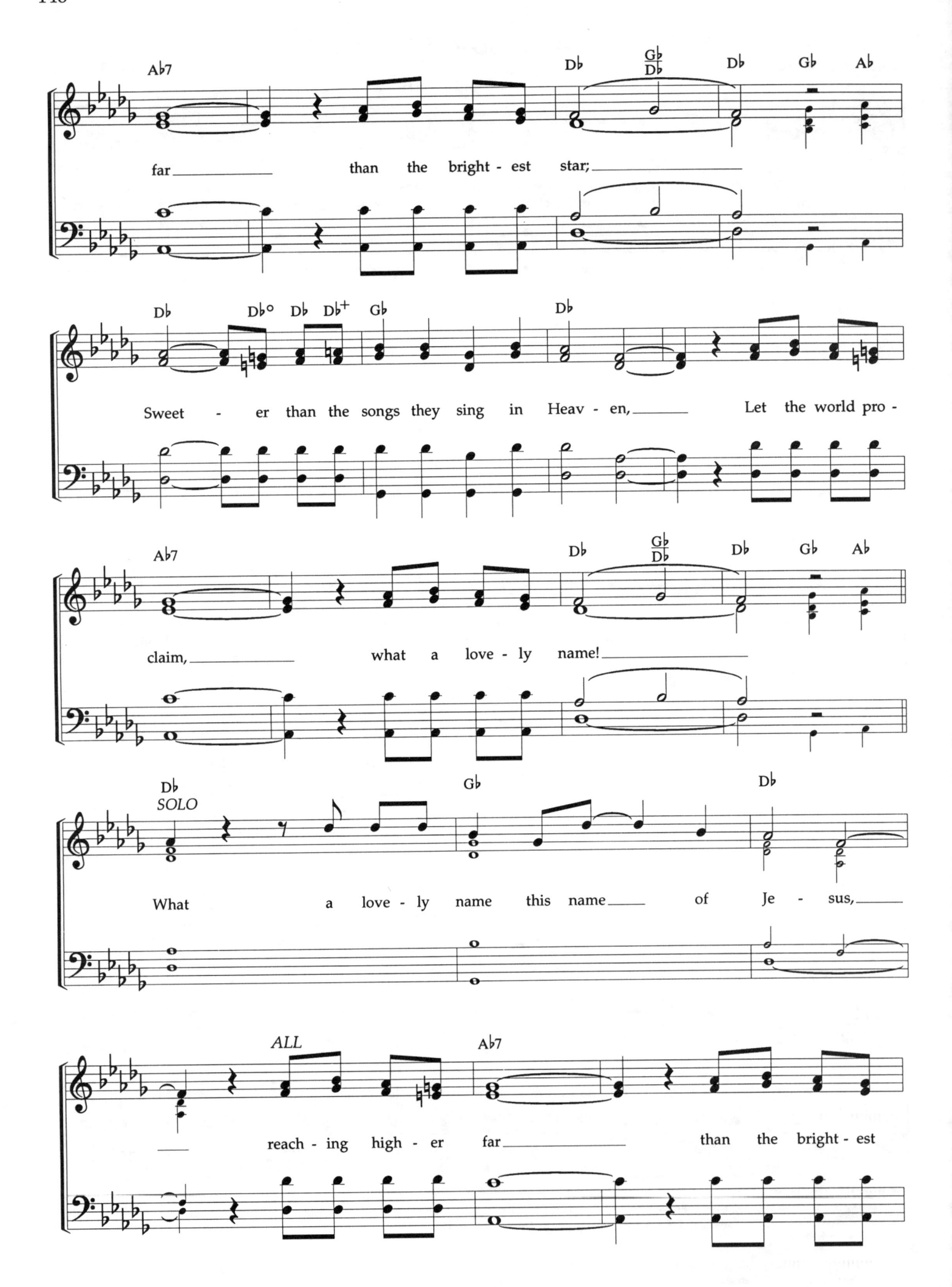

far_____ than the bright-est star;_____ Sweet-er than the songs they sing in Heav-en,_____ Let the world pro-claim,_____ what a love-ly name!_____

SOLO What a love-ly name this name_____ of Je-sus,_____

ALL reach-ing high-er far_____ than the bright-est

Hovie Lister and The Statesmen Quartet

The Sun's Coming Up

Dee Gaskin

Dee Gaskin

1. Once a-gain I faced Sa-tan this morn-ing,___ And I bat-tled him all the day___ long;___ But___ in my weak-ness God sent___ re-in-force-ments,___ And at sun-down I sang___ vic-to-ry's song.___

2. In a world filled with doubts___ and con-fu-sion,___ It's so hard when you don't un-der-stand;___ Oh,___ but I'll stand on a sol-id foun-da-tion,___ And I'll hold to an un-chang-ing___ hand.___

CHORUS

And the sun's com-ing___ up in the morn-ing,___ Ev-'ry tear___ will be

© Copyright 1977 by Rex Nelon Music. All rights reserved. Used by permission of Integrated Copyright Group, Inc..

gone_____ from my eyes;_____ This old clay's gon - na give way to glo - ry,_____ And like an ea - gle, I'll take to the sky._____

Little Troy Lumpkin

We Shall Behold Him

D. R.
Dottie Rambo

1. The sky shall un-fold, pre-par-ing His en-trance; The stars shall ap-plaud Him with thun-ders of praise. The sweet light in His eyes shall en-hance those a-wait-ing; And we shall be-hold Him then face to face.

2. The an-gel shall sound the shout of His com-ing; The sleep-ing shall rise from their slum-ber-ing place. And those who re-main shall be changed in a mo-ment; And we shall be-hold Him then face to face.

CHORUS

And we shall be-hold Him,

© Copyright 1980 by John T. Benson Publishing Co. All rights reserved. Used by permission.

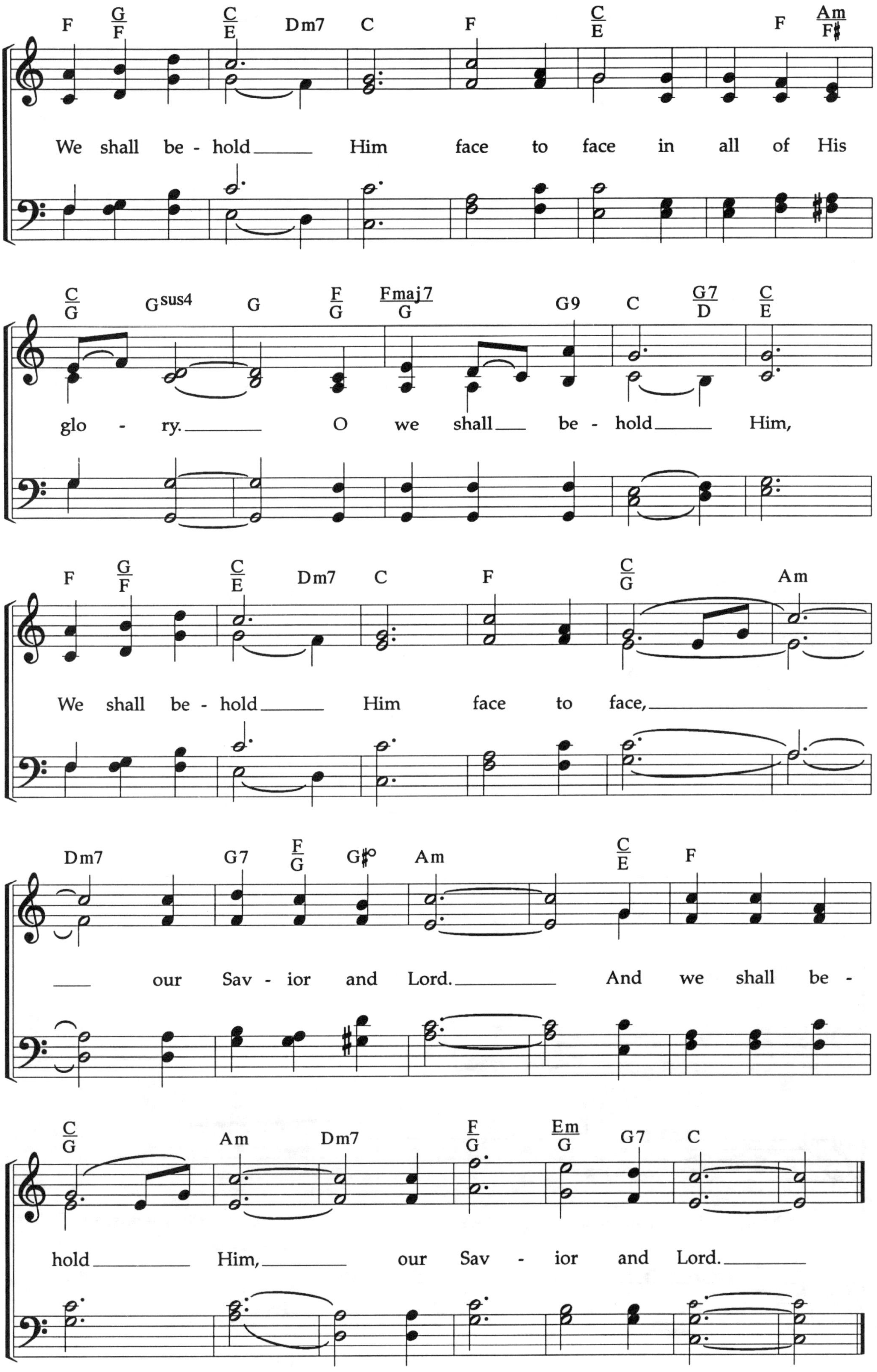
F G/F C/E Dm7 C F C/E F Am/F♯
We shall be - hold Him face to face in all of His
C/G Gsus4 G F/G Fmaj7/G G9 C G7/D C/E
glo - ry. O we shall be - hold Him,
F G/F C/E Dm7 C F C/G Am
We shall be - hold Him face to face,
Dm7 G7 F/G G♯° Am C/E F
our Sav - ior and Lord. And we shall be -
C/G Am Dm7 F/G Em/G G7 C
hold Him, our Sav - ior and Lord.

Time Has Made A Change

H. F.
Harkins Frye

1. Time has made a change since my child-hood day. Many of my friends have gone away. Some I nev-er-more in this life shall see. Time has made a change in me.

2. In my child-hood day I was well and strong. I could climb the hill-side all day long. I am not to-day what I used to be. Time has made a change in me.

3. When I reach my home in that land some-where, Meet my friends that wait me o-ver there; Free from pain and care I shall ev-er be,

CHORUS

Time has made a change in the old home-place. Time has made a change in each smil-ing face; And I know my friends can

© Copyright 1948, renewed 1976 Stamps Quartet Music.
All rights reserved. Used by permission of Integrated Copyright Group, Inc.

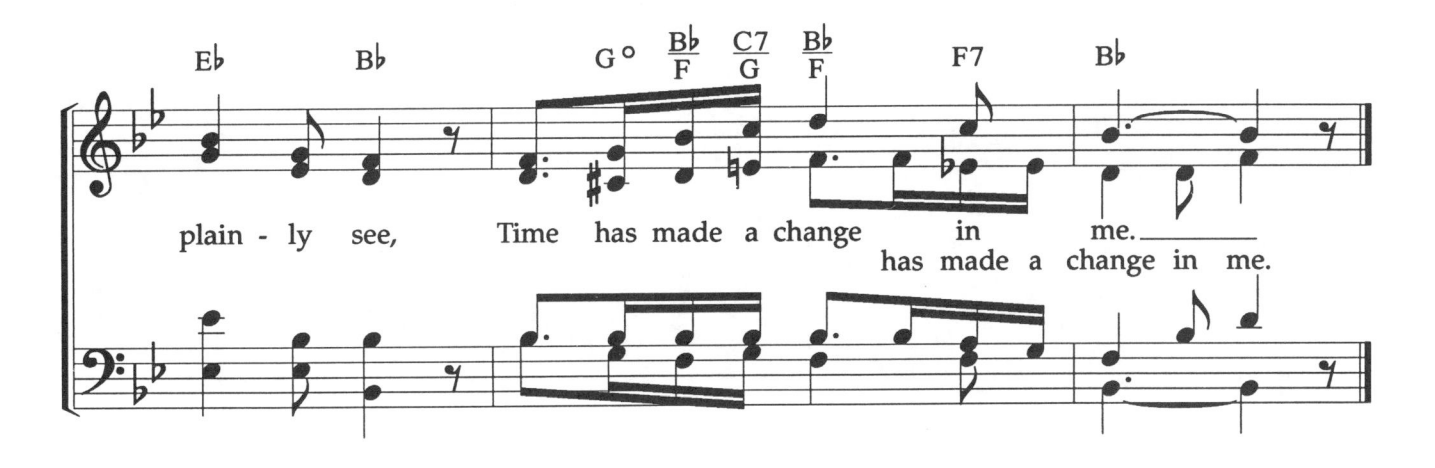

plain-ly see, Time has made a change in me.
has made a change in me.

Hovie Lister and The Statesmen on stage at the historic Ryman Auditorium with Bobby Strickland on tenor and Bervin Kendrick on baritone...Jake on lead and The Big Chief on bass

HOVIE LISTER'S
STATESMEN QUARTET
Favorite Gospel Songs

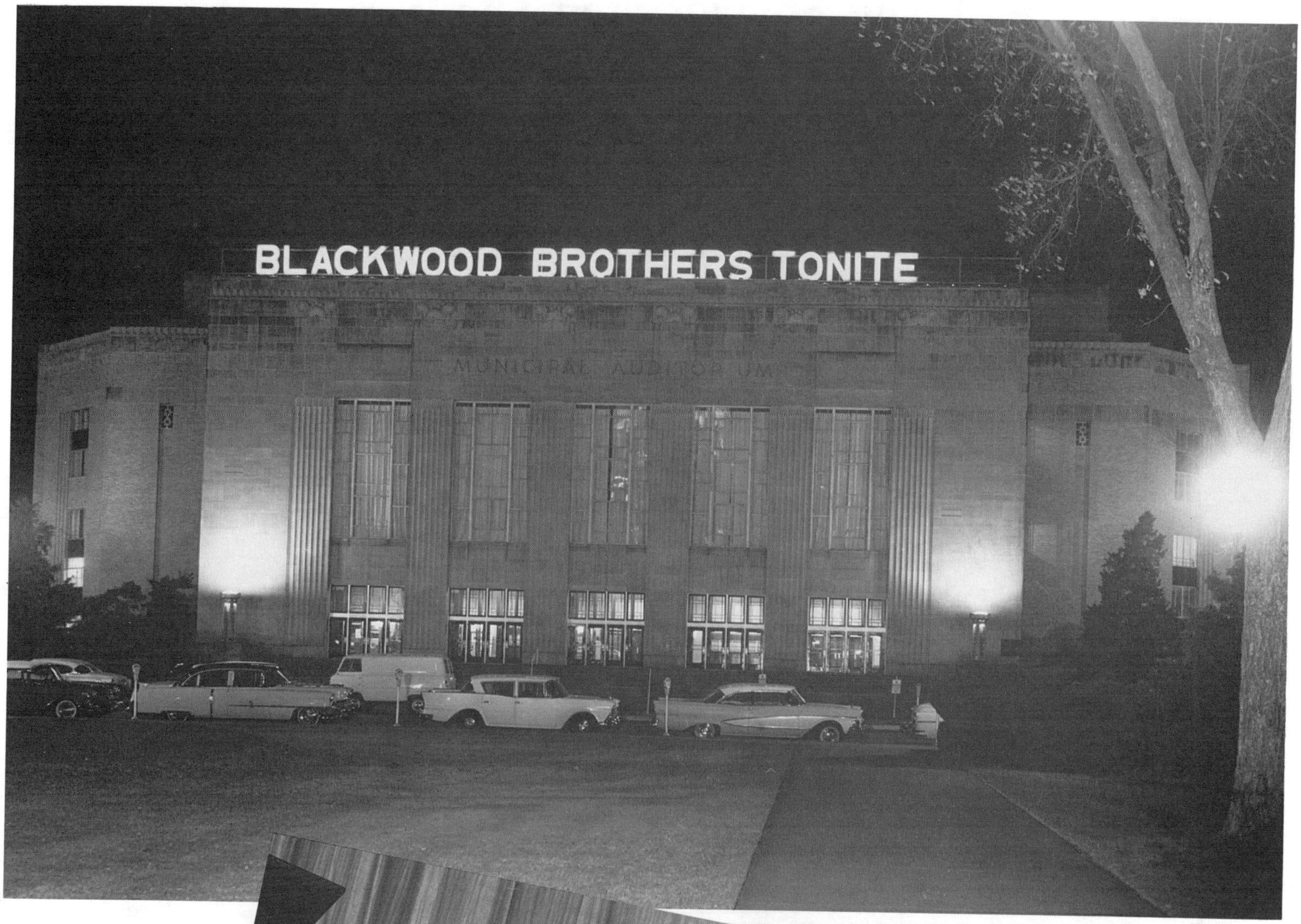
BLACKWOOD BROTHERS TONITE
MUNICIPAL AUDITORIUM

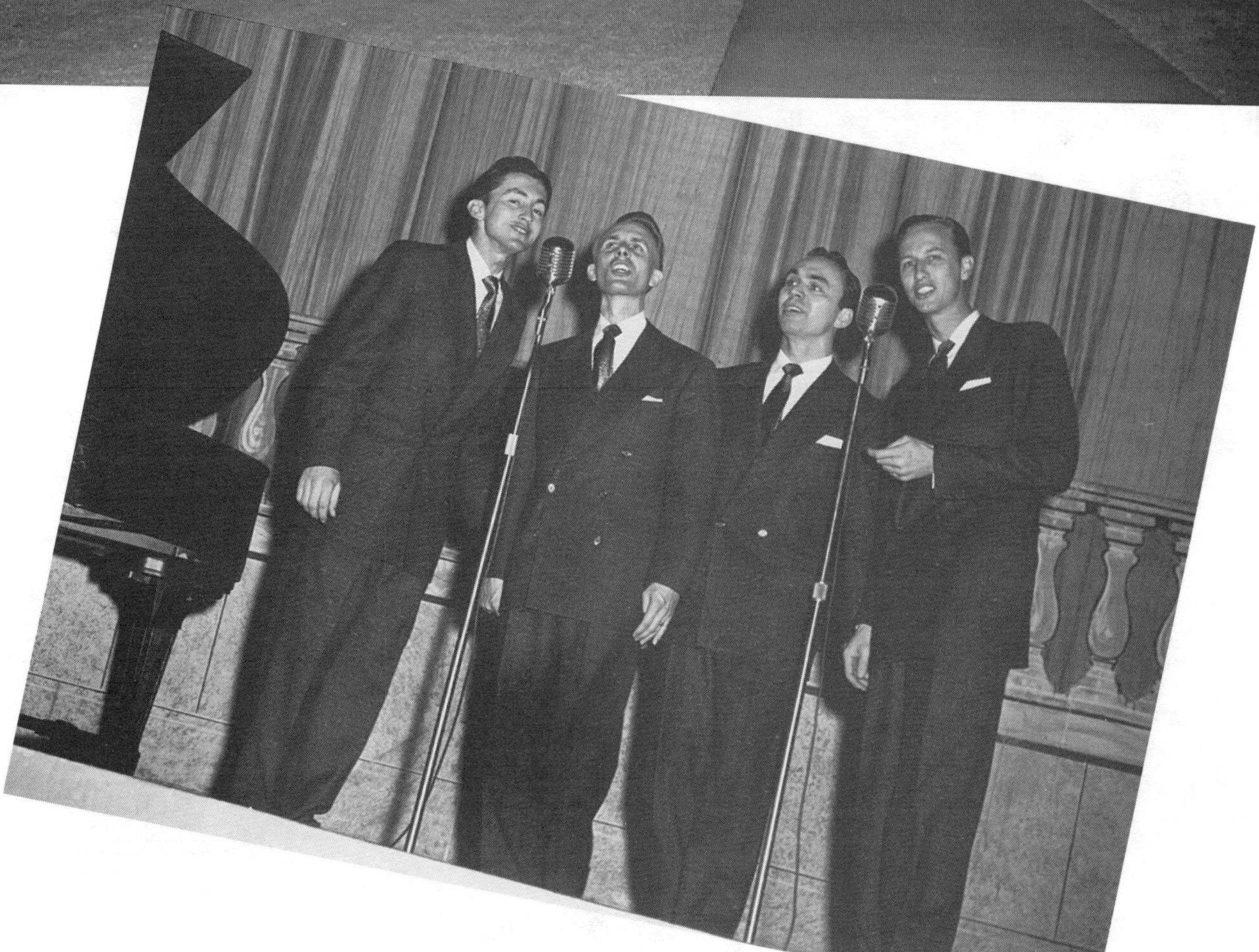

The Answer's On The Way

Charles Goodman / Charles Goodman

1. Many times I bowed beneath a heavy load.
On bended knees to God a prayer I prayed; As I knelt there on the floor, He reminded me once more that the answer is already on the way.

2. If there's a special need within your life, my friend, And you're seeking for an answer ev'ry day; If by faith you'll start believing, mighty soon you'll be receiving, for the answer is already on the way.

CHORUS
Oh, yes, the answer's on the way, this I know.

Je - sus said it, I be - lieve it and it's so;
My Heav-en-ly Fa-ther knows the need be-fore we pray,
And we can rest as-sured the an-swer's on the way.

The John Daniel Quartet

We Have This Moment

Gloria Gaither
William J. Gaither

1. Hold tight to the sound of the music of living, Happy songs from the laughter of children at play; Hold my hand as we run through the sweet fragrant meadows, Making mem'ries of what was today.

2. Tiny voice that I hear is my little girl calling for Daddy to hear just what she has to say; My little son running by the hillside may never be quite like today.

3. Tender words, gentle touch, and a good cup of coffee, And someone that loves me and wants me to stay; Hold them near while they're here, and don't wait for tomorrow, to look back and wish for today.

4. Take the blue of the sky and the green of the forest and the gold and the brown of the freshly mown hay, Add the pale shades of spring and the circus of autumn, and weave you a lovely today.

© Copyright 1975 William J. Gaither. All rights reserved.

For we have this moment to hold in our hands, And to touch as it slips through our fingers like sand; Yesterday's gone, and tomorrow may never come, but we have this moment today.

The Speers singing at Bill Lyles and R.W. Blackwood's funeral

Wedding Day 1962

When Did I Start to Love You?

Does love have a beginning that a meeting's measured by? Does it happen in a moment like white lightning from the sky? Can you tell me its dimensions — just this wide and just this high? When did I start to love you?

Tell me just how many dates it takes for love to really start? And just how many kisses will turn "love" into an art? When does the magic moment come to give away your heart? When did I start to love you?

Was the day we talked of Browning the beginning of it all? Or the time we walked the meadow and the fields of corn so tall that we felt like naughty children hiding from their mother's call? When did I start to love you?

I remember just how timidly your first new song you shared—and by the way you grinned, I knew that you were glad you'd dared, although my evaluation wasn't worth much, still you cared. When did I start to love you?

Was it when I went to meet you in a gown of snowy white? Was it when we signed the license and drove off into the night? Was it when I gave myself to you and felt that it was right? When did I start to love you?

When I feared you wouldn't love me if you knew how I'd been wrong, and I spent a week in mis'ry, but you'd known it all along, and you loved me 'cause you love me, and not because I'm strong! Was it then I came to love you?

Was it when we knew for certain 'bout the baby on the way? Did it start the day you told me I looked pretty—shaped that way? Or did something special happen as we waited that last day... When did I start to love you?

Did it happen when we held her in our arms for the first time? Was it later when I nursed her, this creation—yours and mine? And I knew compared to what we held the world's not worth a dime! When did I start to love you?

There were nights we stayed and prayed by babies, fevers burning hot, when we really didn't know if they would make it through or not—then we'd face the dawn's beginning, thanking God for what we've got—When did I start to love you?

Was it rushing to the clinic with a bone in Amy's throat? Was it nights you saw me shivering and wrapped me in your coat? Was it when I cleaned your bureau drawer and found you'd saved my note—When did I start to love you?

Was it when I saw you showing Benjy how to be a man? How to sheath his strength in meekness—how to gently take a stand—how that only strength of character can salvage this old land? When did I start to love you?

When you held me close in silence when there were no words for grief—when the line of empty caskets gaped at all I called "belief"—when the 'Amen' was so final. I had you, and dared to leave—Was it then I came to love you?

What is the stuff love's made of that can cause the world to glow? Is it that you made the segments that I brought you, well and whole? Was it when I came to recognize the poet in your soul that I began to love you?

It's not of lace and chocolate that valentines are made—All such things are lovely but disintegrate and fade. But love—when once it grows to be—is richer far than jade—I only know— "I love you!"

Gloria Gaither

© Copyright 1977 by Gloria Gaither. All rights reserved.

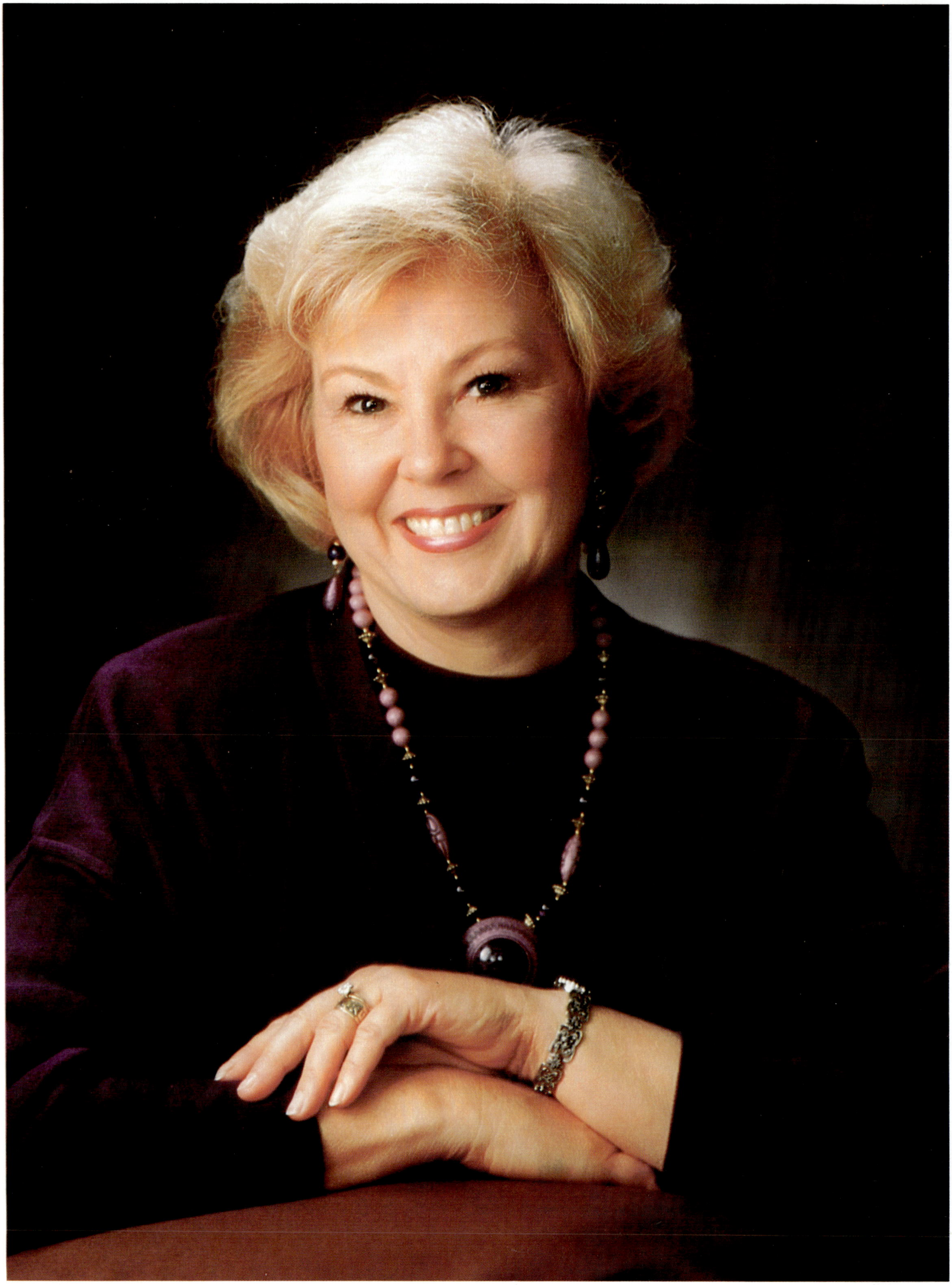

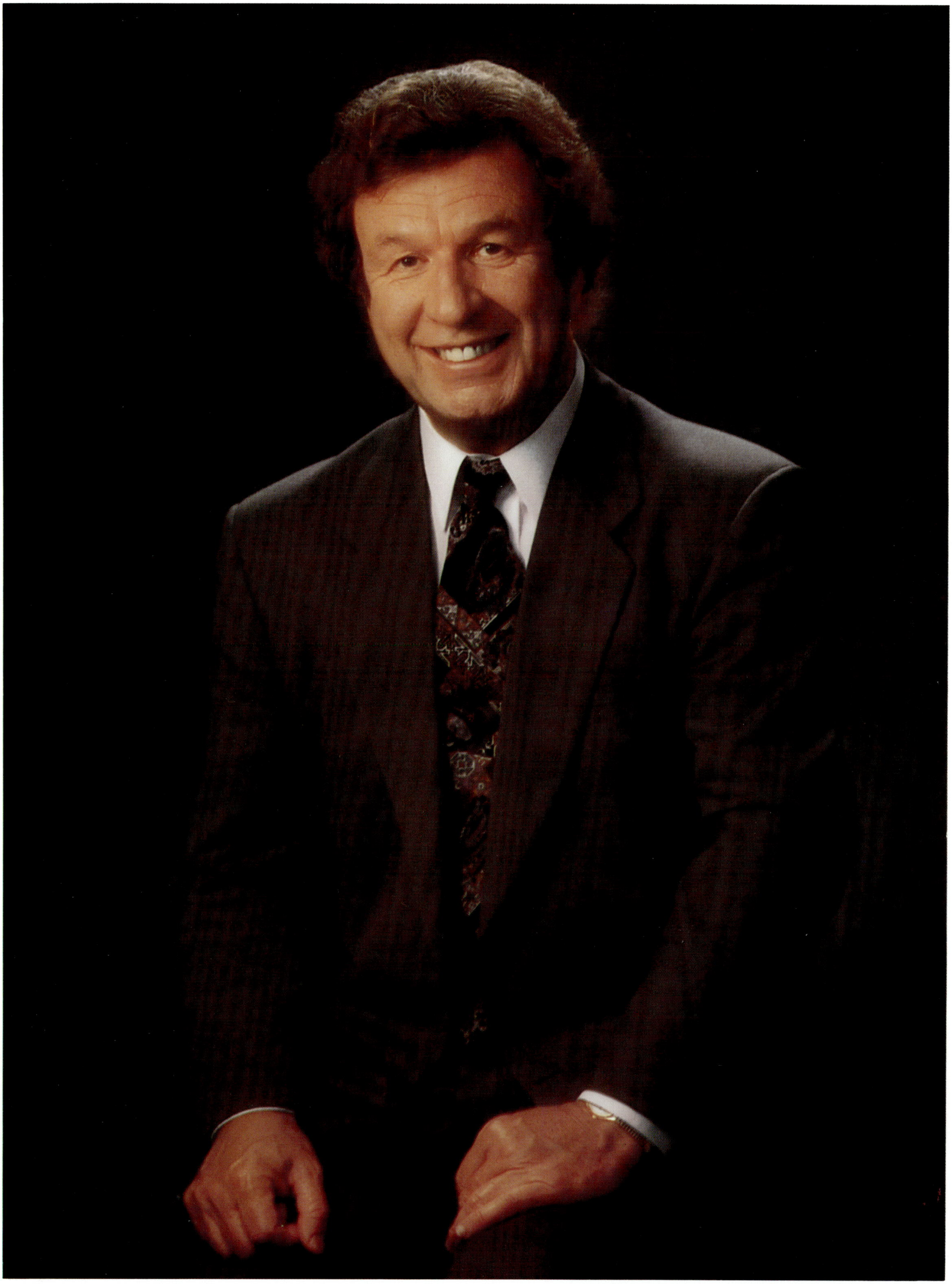

No Sweeter Fellowship

Hear The Voice Of My Beloved

Gloria Gaither
William J. Gaither & Ron Griffin

1. Hear the voice of my Be-lov-ed, gently call at close of day, "Come, my love; oh, come and meet me. Rise, oh rise and come a-way." "Come, my love; oh, come and meet me. Rise, oh, rise and come a-way!"

2. Win-ter's dark will soon be o-ver and the rains are near-ly done; Flow-ers bloom and trees are bud-ding, time for sing-ing has be-gun. Flow-ers bloom and trees are bud-ding, time for sing-ing has be-gun.

3. I have wait-ed through the shad-ows for my Lord to call for me; Now the morn-ing breaks e-ter-nal; In its light His face I see. Now the morn-ing breaks e-ter-nal, and at last His face I see.

4. When you see the fig tree bud-ding, you will know the sum-mer's near. When you hear the words I've spo-ken, you will know my com-ing's near. Keep on list-'ning my be-lov-ed, for my com-ing's ver-y near.

© Copyright 1985 by Gaither Music Company and Ariose Music (admin. by EMI Christian Music Publishing). All rights reserved.

Get Away, Jordan

TRADITIONAL

promised the Lord__ if He'd set me free,__ Well,__ oh,__
One of these mornin's and it won't be long,__ Yes, I want to cross o-ver to
Ooo,_____

I'd__ go un-til I find what the end might be.__
you're gonna look_ for_ me, child, and I'll be gone.__
see my Lord._ Ooo,_____ Yes, I

want to cross o-ver to see my Lord._ Ooo,__
One_ day, one day_ I was
Just a few more ris-ings and

walk-in' a-long,__ I know that__
set-tings of the sun. All my
Yes, I want to cross o-ver to see my Lord._

I__ heard a voice but I saw no one.__
bat-tles will be fought and my vic-t'ries won.__
Ooo,_____ Yes, I want to cross

o - ver to see my Lord. The voice I heard sound-ed,
All the friends that I used to
Ooo,

oh, so sweet,
love so dear, Yes, I want to cross o-ver to see my Lord. Came
Well, now they've

down from my head to the sole of my feet.
gone on to glo-ry and left me here.
Ooo,
Oh, Yes, I want to cross o-ver to

see my Lord. well, Oh, want to cross o-ver to see my Lord.

When my feet get cold, eyes are shut, bod-y been

chilled by the hand of death,___ tongue___ glued to the roof of my mouth,___ hands lay fold-ed a-cross my breast,___ Don't have to wor-ry 'bout the way I fair,___ God Al-might-y done told me that He'd be right there___ to lift me up on His wings of love,___ car-ry my soul___ to the heav-ens up a-bove, Tell me Jor-dan's, deep and wide,___ But I prom - ised Moth - er I'd meet her on the oth - er side, So,

get a - way! _____ Oh, get a - way! _____ Get a - way,
Get a - way Jor - dan! ____

___ Get a - way back, oh, chil - ly Jor - dan, I
oh, chil - ly Jor - dan, Get back, get back, Jor - dan,

1.
Gb   Db
want to cross o - ver to see my Lord; ____ Oh,

2.
Gb   Db
want to cross o - ver to see my Lord. _____

Jake Hess and The Imperials

The Happy Goodmans

I Thank My Savior For It All

Lee Roy Abernathy   Lee Roy Abernathy

1. There's a mil-lion things I'd like to do to serve my Lord, There's a mil-lion sin-ful plea-sures I can-not af-ford; All the world-ly things I might a-chieve tho' great or small, I will thank my God be-cause I know He owns it all.
2. I re-mem-ber well those wast-ed years when sin-sick tossed, I can still re-call those aw-ful words, "Your soul is lost"; Then the love of God came down and sanc-ti-fied my soul, Ev-er since that day I'm glad to say I've been made whole.
3. When the time shall come for me to go to meet my King, When it seems that I can al-most hear the home bells ring; I shall then re-view the world-ly deeds that I have done, And will thank my God that he con-duct-ed ev-'ry one.

CHORUS

When the sun goes down, I thank my God, In the fall or spring, I thank my God, When it

When the sun goes down and night-time falls, I thank my God, In the fall or spring for ev-'ry thing, I thank my God, When it

© Copyright 1944 (renewal 1971) Tennessee Music and Printing./ASCAP, a div. of Pathway Music, P.O. Box 2250, Cleveland, TN 37320 in <u>Songs</u> <u>Forever</u>. Used by permission.

seems like trou - bles turn me a - side, I can ask for
seems like trou - ble comes a - long to turn me a - side, I can ask for help and

help, I'll not be de - nied; When it seems my
rest as - sured I'll not be de - nied; When it seems like all the

work has been in vain, Then I think the price when
work I've done has been in vain, Then I think of what a price was paid when

Christ was slain, Ev - 'ry morn - ing, eve - ning, noon, or night, mat - ters not what

may be - fall, I will sing and thank my Sav - ior for it all.
 I will sing God's praise

I'm Free Again

V. B. (Vep) Ellis

1. Sa-tan led my soul a-stray (Sa-tan led my soul a-stray, I drift-ed),
2. On the sin-ful path be-low (on the sin-ful path be-low is trou-ble),
3. Soon the pearl-y gates I'll see (soon the pearl-y gates I'll see in Heav-en),

From the straight and nar-row way (that leads to hap-pi-ness and life e-
All in sor-row, grief and woe, (the sin-ner's load is might-y hard to
Soon I'll live e-ter-nal-ly (And then I'll nev-er die but live for-

ter-nal); But to Je-sus I did pray, (to the Lord I hum-bly prayed),
car-ry); But I've left the shift-ing sand, (I have left the shift-ing sand),
ev-er); Friends and loved ones wait for me, (friends and loved ones wait for me),

He heard my prayer,___ res-cued me that ver-y day, (that ver-y day).
Up-on the Rock,___ sol-id Rock, I'll take my stand, (I'll take my stand).
I'll sail up high,___ through the sky, be-cause I'm free, (be-cause I'm free).

© Copyright 1948 Stamps Quartet Music, renewed 1976 by Stamps Quartet Music.
All rights reserved. Used by permission of Integrated Copyright Group, Inc.

171

CHORUS

Praise God I'm free, I've been set free by the grace of God; I'm free, with a settled peace within, No more the paths of sin I trod; I'm free, Heaven's gates I'll enter in, The blood has cleansed ev'ry sinful stain; I'm free, I'm free again.

Free from ev'ry chain of sin, Praise the living God, I'm free again.

O Happy Day

Philip Doddridge   Arr. by L. B. Harris

1. O happy day that fixed my choice
On Thee, my Savior and my God! (the living God!)
Well may this glowing heart rejoice,
And tell its raptures all abroad. (abroad.)

2. O happy bond that seals my vows
To Him who merits all my love! (yes, all my love!)
Let cheerful anthems fill His house,
While to that sacred shrine I move. (I move.)

3. 'Tis done, the great transaction's done!
I am my Lord's and He is mine! (He's truly mine!)
He drew me and I followed on,
Charmed to confess the voice divine. (divine.)

CHORUS
C/G C C/G C9 F A7/E Dm
He taught me how to watch and pray,
He taught me how to pray, to watch and pray,
He taught me how to pray, to watch and pray,
He taught me how to pray, to watch and pray,
Am A♭ C/G C9 F
And live re - joic - ing ev - 'ry day;
And live re - joic - ing ev - 'ry day;
And live re - joic - ing ev - 'ry pass - ing day;
And live re - joic - ing ev - 'ry pass - ing day;
B♭/F F
O hap - py day, O hap - py day,
O hap - py day, O hap - py day,
O hal - le - lu - jah! O hap - py
Hap - py day, blest hap - py
A7/E Dm F/A F/C C7 F B♭/F F
When Je - sus washed my sins a - way.
When Je - sus washed my sins a - way, my sins a - way.
day When Je - sus washed my sins a - way, my sins a - way.
day, When Je - sus washed my sins a - way.

My Home

Lee Roy Abernathy

1. Mid the toil and strife of this old life, my mind still wanders back
To my childhood days and things that used to be;
In a care-free way I'd romp and play, I wish those days were back,
Still my thoughts are filled with pleasant memories.

2. Not a day goes by that I don't try to help some child along,
For I still recall what others did for me;
With my Dad so near, and Mother dear, I soon learned right from wrong,
Maybe that's what makes me love this melody.

3. I believe a home can raise a child, and it will not depart,
Leading them to God is up to Mom and Dad;
So if I should stray, and lose my way, 'twould make them both so sad,
For they gave me ev'ry blessing that they had.

CHORUS
What a time I had with my Mom and Dad,
I had a home sweet

© Copyright 1946 Abernathy Publishing, renewed 1974 Abernathy Publishing.
All rights reserved. Used by permission of Integrated Copyright Group, Inc..

G7 G+ Bm/A G7/B C9 C7
I can still re - mem - ber, I'm so glad that I've
home, I'll ne'er for - get
F7 B♭ E♭m/B♭ B♭ N.C.
not for - got - ten those days.
those days. 'Twas in my
B♭ D D7 G7
With the help of Dad, and the friends we had, and my dear old
home I learned
G+ Bm/A G7/B C9 F7
Moth - er, That's the rea - son now, I am sing - ing God's
to sing the Mas - ter's
B♭ E♭m/B♭ B♭ B♭9 Gm/C B♭7/D E♭ E♭9 E♭m B♭
praise. In vis - ion now I see the fam - 'ly al - tar,

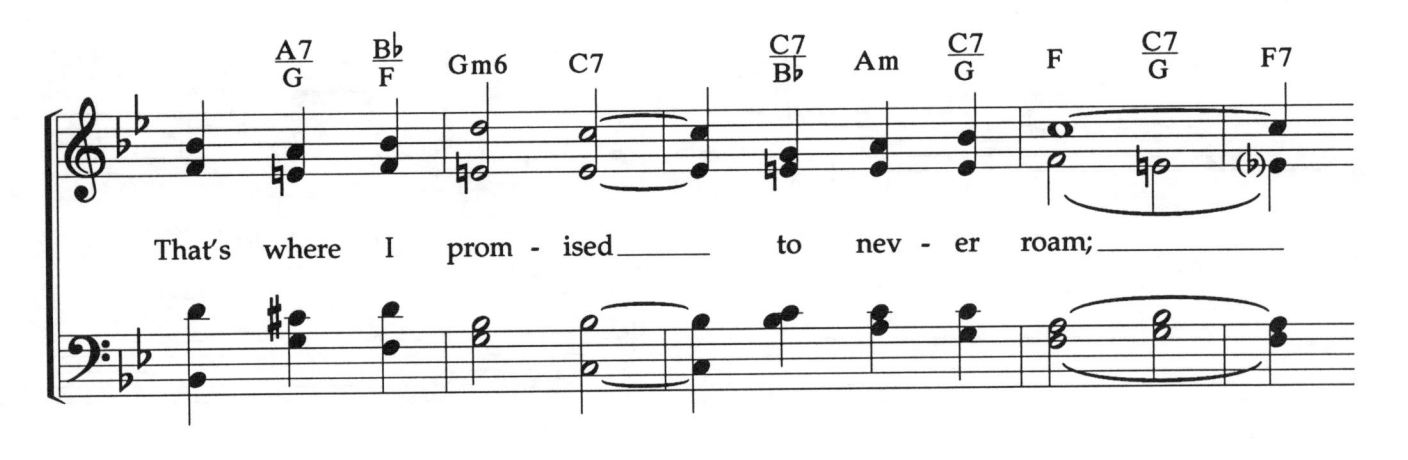

That's where I prom - ised to nev - er roam;
God bless my Dad - dy Fill my Dad with cheer, and my Moth - er dear,
and for they both still love you, For the
my Moth - er for
priv - i - lege of a won - der - ful home.
our Chris - tian home.

A Newborn Feeling

L. R. A.
Lee Roy Abernathy

1. Got a lot to tell you 'bout the Lord to-day,— How He took me in and washed my sins a-way;— Filled me with the Spir-it and a-maz-ing grace,— Prom-ised me a man-sion and a rest-ing place;— Told me how the an-gel band would shout and sing,— How we're gon-na make the hills and val-leys ring;— May-be that's the rea-son that I

2. When I stop and think a-bout the pres-ent day,— How the world-ly peo-ple pass the time a-way,— Makes me kind-a won-der what the fu-ture holds,— How we're gon-na ev-er reach the sin-ful souls;— We can on-ly reach them if we kneel and pray,— Try to draw a pic-ture of the judg-ment day;— Live a life be-fore them that will

© Copyright by Abernathy Publishing. All rights reserved. Used by permission of Integrated Copyright Group, Inc.

feel so fine,___ All my wea-ry trou-bles have been left be-hind.___
tes-ti-fy,___ Prove you have the bless-ing from the Lord on high.___

CHORUS

I've got a new-born feel-ing dwell-ing in my heart to-day,___

Be-cause the love___ of Je-sus came in-to my heart to stay;___ I nev-er re-al-ized___ that I had lost___ my way,___ Un-til the love of Je-sus washed my sins a-way,___

I've got a new-born feeling in my heart today.

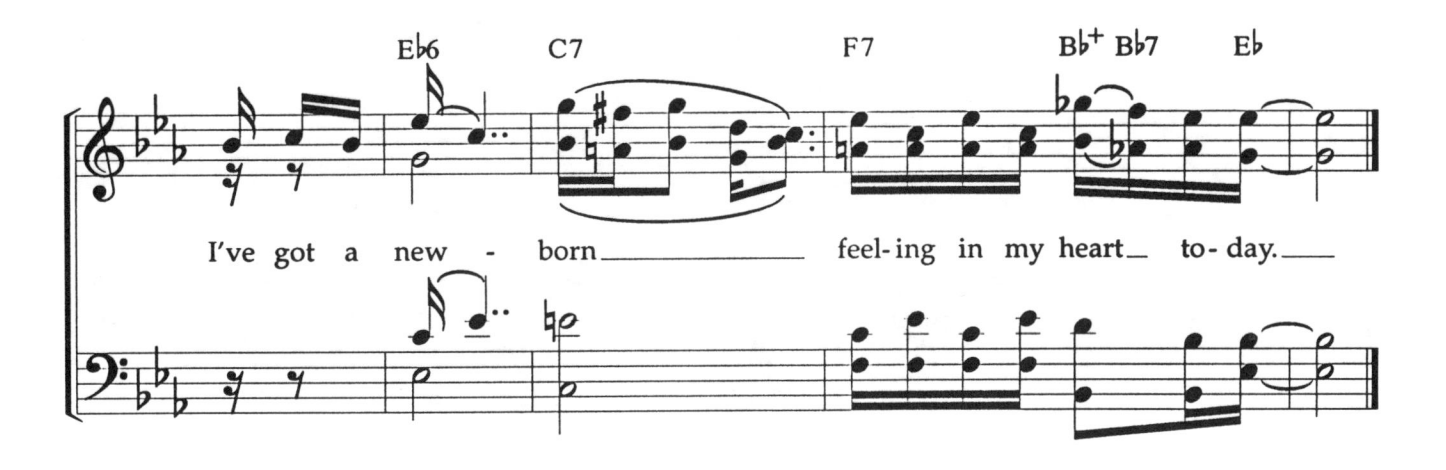

The LeFevre Trio with Jim Waite

I Need No Mansion Here

C. S. G.
C. S. Grogan

1. When bur-dens come so hard to bear, that no earth-ly friend can share; Tears drive a-way the smiles and leave my heart in pain. — Then my Lord from Heav'n a-bove speaks to me in tones of love; Wipes the tears a-way and makes me smile a-gain.

2. Oh, the thought to me is sweet, that my loved ones I will meet; — At the end-ing of the jour-ney here be-low. — Seems I hear their voic-es blend, in a world with-out an end; I won't wor-ry when the time shall come to go.

3. When Je-sus comes to claim His own, I will move to my new home; I'll walk and talk with Him up-on the streets of gold. — A man-sion there is wait-ing me, soon its beau-ty I will see; In that Cit-y where we nev-er shall grow old.

CHORUS

I need no man-sion here be-low, for Je-sus said that I could

© Copyright assigned 1953 Gospel Tone Music Publications. All rights reserved. Used by permission.

go, to a home be-yond the clouds not made with hands.

Won't you come and go a-long? We will sing the sweet-est

song, ev-er played up-on the harps in glo-ry-land.

The Statesmen singing at the funeral of R.W. Blackwood and Bill Lyles

Lord, I'm Ready Now To Go

Lee Roy Abernathy
Lee Roy Abernathy

1. There's a Cit-y on high, far be-yond the blue sky, a par-a-dise I'm told; Such a won-der-ful place, for the ran-somed by grace, and none shall e'er grow old.
2. Now's the time to do right, morn-ing, eve-ning and night, for we'll be judged some day; There in Heav-en a-bove we shall sing of His love, while a-ges roll a-way.

CHORUS

Oh, that land of joy and won-der-ful beau-ty Where I know my friends and loved ones a-wait; Day by day I know I'm do-ing my

Oh, that land of beau-ty rare where all my friends and loved ones now are pa-tient-ly wait-ing, Ev-'ry-day my

© Copyright 1943, renewed 1971 by Abernathy Publishing Company.
All rights reserved. Used by permission of Integrated Copyright Group, Inc..

Dm/C C A9
du - ty, I can hard - ly wait to en - ter the
du - ty do, It seems that I can hard - ly
D7 G Dm G Dm G
gate; Seems I al - most hear those wel - come bells
wait to en - ter that home - land; Seems I al - most
Dm/C C A7
ring - ing, I'm just wait - ing for the trum - pet to
hear the glad bells ring - ing, I'm just wait - ing
D D+ G Dm G Dm
blow, How I long to join that won - der - ful
till the trum - pet sound - eth, Soon I'll join that
Dm/C C G° G E° G/D A7 D7 G
sing - ing, Lord, I'm read - y now to go.
cho - rus grand, such sing - ing, Lord, I'm read - y now to go.

I Believe In The Old Time Way

J.D.S.
J. D. Sumner

In this modern day of living, my, how things have changed.
People often get religion, but their heart's not changed.
They go to church, they testify, but what an awful fate,
to find they have no real salvation, but will be too late.

CHORUS

Well, I went down to an old camp-meeting,

© Copyright 1959, renewed 1987 by Gospel Quartet Music.
All rights reserved. Used by permission of Integrated Copyright Group, Inc.

F9 Gm/B♭ B♭7 A♭/B♭ E♭
I prayed through in the old - time way.
B♭7 E♭ E♭/D♭ C7
Oh, it was there at an old - time al - tar,
F9 Gm/B♭ B♭7 A♭/B♭ E♭
I was saved by a - maz - ing grace.
A♭7 E♭
I con-fessed my sin - ful liv - ing, I was sor - ry for my sins.
F E♭/F F7 E♭/F F7 B♭7
I o - pened up my heart to Heav - en, then my God came in.

186

It was there at an old-time at an old-time al-
there at an old-time al-tar, yes, I was saved by a-maz-ing
tar, I was saved by a-maz-ing grace. Well, I be-
grace.
lieve, be-lieve, be-lieve, in the old-time way.
I be-lieve, be-lieve, be-lieve that's what it's gon-na

take. Well, I be - lieve, be - lieve, be - lieve, in the old - time way. I be - lieve, be - lieve, be - lieve He'll take me home to stay.

The Jordanaires

Led Out Of Bondage

Robert L. Prather

Robert L. Prather

Verses are to be spoken rhythmically.

Wah - oo - wah - oo - wah - oo, Wah - oo - wah - oo - wah - oo, Wah - oo - wah - oo - wah - oo, Wah - oo - wah - oo - wah - oo, Wah - oo,

1. God's children were slaves in E-gypt's land, so God took Moses by the hand, said, "Moses, tell old Pharaoh to set 'em free." But Moses wanted a way to get out, cause in His mind he's be-gin-ning to doubt, He said, "Lord, old Pharaoh
2. Now the Lord said, "Moses, I've got pow'r and I'll be with you ev-'ry hour, Now go tell Pharaoh to set My children free." But Moses did and the Lord helped out, He sent the plagues through the land a-bout, till Pharaoh told 'em to
3. When they came to the banks of the ocean blue, they turned to Moses, said, "What-'ll we do?" and Moses fell to his knees there in the sand. Then the Lord said, "Moses, trust in God, why all you got-ta do is raise that rod and o-ver those might-y

© Copyright 1949 Peer International Corp. Copyright renewed. All rights reserved. Used by permission.

Wah - oo, / ain't gon-na lis-ten to me." Wah,____ Wah - oo -
go and__ let__ him be. Well, the Lord said, "Son,___ throw___
wa-ters__ stretch_ your hand." So they start-ed out___ with a
So,___ Mos-es fol-lowed the___

wah-oo-wah-oo, Wah - oo - wah-oo-wah-oo,
down that rod," so,___ Mos-es did,___ then he cried to God 'cause it
cloud by day, and a fire by night___ to___ lead the way till old
Lord's com-mand, and the wa-ters part-ed and there in the sand they___

Wah - oo-wah-oo-wah-oo, Wah-oo-wah-oo-wah-oo,
turned to a snake___ as___ e-vil and wick-ed as sin, Then he
Phar-aoh__ sud-den-ly de-cid-ed to change__ his mind, So he
saw a__ path that__ led__ to the oth-er shore, Well, the

Wah - oo-wah-oo-wah-oo, Wah - oo -
cried a-gain with__ an aw-ful wail for the Lord said, "Seize__ him__
gath-ered to-geth-er his sol-dier band, got__ all the char-i-ots through-
ground__ was dry and they passed on through, so__ Phar-aoh's ar-my tho't__

wah - oo - wah - oo, Wah - oo, Wah - oo,
by the tail," so,_ Mos - es did_ and it turned_ to a rod a - gain.
out the land, said, "I'll let them Is - ra'- lites_ go_ some_ oth - er time."
they would, too, but the wa - ters fell_ and they nev - er was_ seen no more.

CHORUS

Wah.___ God prom-ised to lead His chil-dren out of bond-age,

He said He'd free them from Phar-aoh's e - vil hand;___

He prom-ised to guide and pro-tect them on their jour-ney,___ and lead them

1. 2. to the Prom - ised Land.___ *3.* to the Prom - ised Land.___

Burdens Are Lifted At Calvary

John M. Moore   John M. Moore

1. Days are filled with sor-row and care, Hearts are lone-ly and drear;
2. Cast your care on Je-sus to-day, Leave your wor-ry and fear;
3. Trou-bled soul, the Sav-ior can see Ev-'ry heart-ache and tear;

Bur-dens are lift-ed at Cal-va-ry, Je-sus is ver-y near.
Bur-dens are lift-ed at Cal-va-ry, Je-sus is ver-y near.
Bur-dens are lift-ed at Cal-va-ry, Je-sus is ver-y near.

CHORUS

Bur-dens are lift-ed at Cal-va-ry, Cal-va-ry, Cal-va-ry;

Bur-dens are lift-ed at Cal-va-ry, Je-sus is ver-y near.

© Copyright 1952 and renewal © 1979 by Singspiration Music.
All rights reserved. Used by permission of Benson Music Group, Inc.

Grace Greater Than Our Sin

Julia H. Johnston
Daniel B. Towner

1. Mar-vel-ous grace of our lov-ing Lord, Grace that ex-ceeds our sin and our guilt! Yon-der on Cal-va-ry's mount out-poured— There where the blood of the Lamb was spilt.
2. Sin and de-spair, like the sea-waves cold, Threat-en the soul with in-fi-nite loss; Grace that is great-er— yes, grace un-told— Points to the Ref-uge, the might-y Cross.
3. Dark is the stain that we can-not hide, What can a-vail to wash it a-way? Look! There is flow-ing a crim-son tide— Whit-er than snow you may be to-day.
4. Mar-vel-ous, in-fi-nite, match-less grace, Free-ly be-stowed on all who be-lieve! You that are long-ing to see His face, Will you this mo-ment His grace re-ceive!

CHORUS

Grace, grace, God's grace, Grace that will par-don and cleanse with-in; Grace, grace, God's grace, Grace that is great-er than all our sin!

Hallelujah To The Lamb

Conrad Cook

1. It was told that He would come and the race He would run, It would end on an old rugged cross; But when they laid Him in the tomb, the pow'r of the Lord went in the room, Now He reigns for - ev - er more.

2. Church, He's coming back some day to take us home with Him to stay, Where His glory for - ev - er we will share; And when that first trumpet sounds we will all be glory bound, Up there we'll live for - ev - er -

CHORUS

Hal - le - lu - jah to the Lamb! Hal - le -

© Copyright 1993 Swansound Music. All rights reserved. Used by permission.

lu - jah to the Lamb___ that was slain up - on a tree!___ By His stripes we are healed! By His blood we are sealed! Hal - le - lu - jah to the Lamb___ of God!___

I'll Leave It All Behind

M. L.
Mosie Lister

1. I've been blue the whole day through,— I've been griev-ing all the day.—
2. On this road a heav-y load— I must bear while trudg-ing on,—

Think-ing of the land I love,— makes me want to fly a-way.—
When I fly a-bove the sky,— I will nev-er walk a-lone.—

Down here I walk— in sin and sor-row,— a heav-y load— of care is mine,— But when I leave— for heav-en's Cit-y,— I'll leave it all be-hind.—

© Copyright 1951, renewed 1979 Lillenas Publishing Company.
All rights reserved. Used by permission of Integrated Copyright Group, Inc.

For ev-'ry tear____ and ev-'ry heart-ache, For ev-'ry mile____ that I must roam,____ I'm that much near - er Heav-en's glo-ry____ and my e-ter-nal home;____ Oh, Heav-en's gates____ are stand-ing o-pen.____ I see____ them stand-ing o-pen wide.____ I know there's joy____ and glo-ry wait-ing.____ Oh, how I long to get in-side.____

I'll never shed a tear in Heaven, I'll never grieve, I'll never pine, For when I leave this world of sorrow, I'll leave it all behind.

Ira Stanphill

Two Great Pioneers

Jake Hess
and Hovie Lister

When All Of God's Singers Get Home

Luther G. Presley, Chorus by V. O. S.
Virgil O. Stamps

1. What a song of delight in that City so bright will be wafted 'neath Heaven's fair dome; How the ransomed will raise happy songs in His praise,
2. As we sing here on earth, songs of sadness or mirth, 'tis a foretaste of rapture to come; But our joy can't compare with the glory up there, When all of God's singers get home.
3. Having overcome sin, "hallelujah, amen," will be heard in that land o'er the foam; Ev-'ry heart will be light and each face will be bright,

CHORUS

When all of God's singers get home, where never a sorrow will come; There'll be "no place like
When all of God's singers get home, or heartache will come; There'll be "no place like

© Copyright 1937, renewal 1965 by Stamps-Baxter Music. All rights reserved. Used by permission of Benson Music Group, Inc.

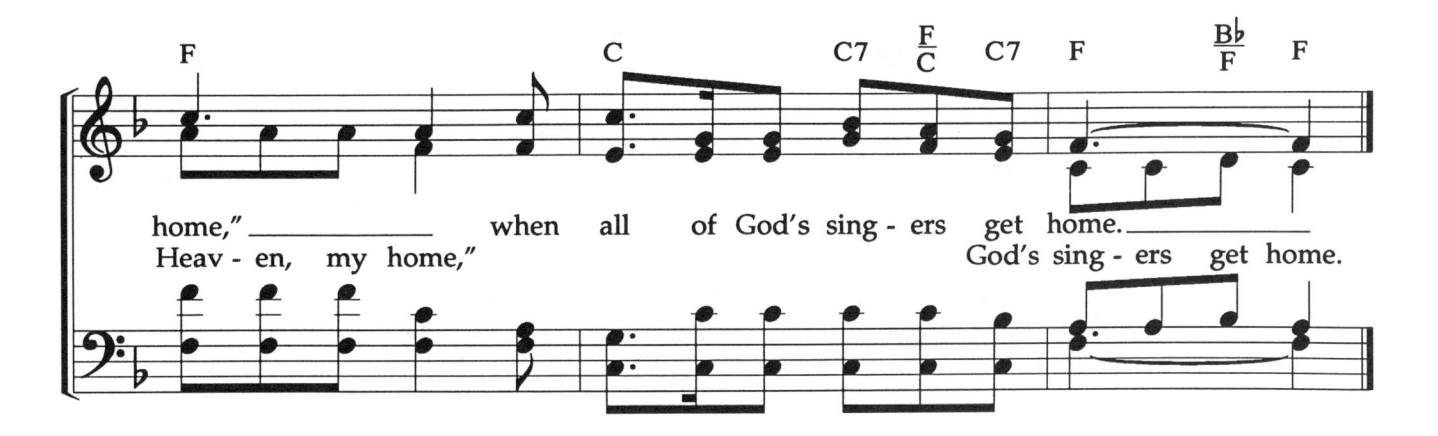

When All Of God's Singers Get Home

    I like to think that before time began, before the world was created or galaxies flung into space, there was God — and He was singing a song. The music was so beautiful that it had to be heard. So God created . . . and down through the ages He's always had His singers who picked up the fragments of the melody, hummed bits of harmony, wrote phrases of poetry, or danced short movements.

    No one has ever heard the whole song since that day God sang it alone. But one of these days He will gather all His children home, and one by one the singers of all the ages will lift their voices and fill in the parts life taught to them. At last we'll hear love's sweetest song as it was first conceived in the heart of the great song writer Himself. It will be perfect. What music there will be when the song of the ages is sung around the Father's throne when all of God's singers get home!

Gloria Gaither

Beyond The Sunset

Virgil P. Brock
Blanche Kerr Brock

1. Be-yond the sun-set, O bliss-ful morn-ing, When with our Sav-ior Heav'n is be-gun; Earth's toil-ing end-ed, O glo-rious dawn-ing, Be-yond the sun-set, when day is done.
2. Be-yond the sun-set no clouds will gath-er, No storms will threat-en, no fears an-noy; O day of glad-ness, O day un-end-ing, Be-yond the sun-set, e-ter-nal joy!
3. Be-yond the sun-set a hand will guide me To God, the Fa-ther, whom I a-dore; His glo-rious pres-ence, His words of wel-come, Will be my por-tion on that fair shore.
4. Be-yond the sun-set, O glad re-un-ion, With our dear loved ones who've gone be-fore; In that fair home-land we'll know no part-ing, Be-yond the sun-set for-ev-er-more!

© Copyright 1936, renewed 1964 by The Rodeheaver Co. (div. of Word, Inc.).
All rights reserved. Used by permission.

Should You Go First And I Remain

Should you go first and I remain to walk the road alone, I'll live in memory's garden, dear, with happy days we've known. In spring I'll watch for roses red when fades the lilac blue, and in early fall when brown leaves call, I'll catch a glimpse of you.

Should you go first and I remain for battles to be fought, each thing you've touched along the way will be a hallowed spot. I'll hear your voice, I'll see your smile and though blindly I may grope, the memory of your helping hand will bore me on with hope; and should you go first and I remain to finish with the scroll, no lengthening shadows shall creep in to make this life seem droll. We've known so much of happiness and we've had our cup of joy, but memory is one gift of God that death cannot destroy.

Should you go first and I remain, one thing I'd have you do: walk slowly down that long, long path for soon I'll follow you, and I'll want to know each step you take that I may walk the same, for someday, someday down that lonely road you'll hear me call your name.

Albert Rowswell

ARTISTS APPEARING IN GAITHER VIDEO SERIES

Doris Akers
1816 4th Avenue, South
Minneapolis, MN 55404

Assurance
P.O. Box 1909
Douglasville, GA 30135
404/489-8853

Billy Blackwood
102 Dillon Drive
Hendersonville, TN 37075
615/824-9077

James Blackwood and
   the James Blackwood Quartet
4411 Sequoia Road
Memphis, TN 38117
901/683-5711

Jimmy Blackwood
P.O. Box 280932
Memphis, TN 38168
800/476-7749

Terry Blackwood
P.O. Box 40921
Nashville, TN 37204
615/386-9552

Ray Boltz
Ray Boltz Music, Inc.
P.O. Box 2562
Muncie, IN 47307
317/286-3065

Bob Cain
3532 Stonehinge Place
Birmingham, AL 35210
205/956-9492

Jack Clark
P.O. Box 5555
Cleveland, TN 37320
615/479-1200

Cynthia Clawson
P.O. Box 6202
San Antonio, TX 78209

Elmer Cole
P.O. Box 331
Lookout Mt., TN 37350
706/820-2356

Dr. H. Frank Collins
4001 88th Place
Lubbock, TX 79423
806/798-2723

The Couriers
   Neil Enloe
   Phil Enloe
   Duane Nicholson
506 E. Winding Hill Road
Mechanicsburg, PA 17055
717/766-2504

Bob Crews
The Harmoneers
8426 Timberlane Drive
Douglasville, GA 30134
404/949-2657

Geron Davis
P.O. Box 8169
Alexandria, LA 71306
318/448-9380

Ken Davis
6080 W. 82nd Drive
Arvada, CO 80003
303/425-1319

The Dixie Melody Boys
513 Harding Avenue
Kinston, NC 28501
919/523-9306

Jessy Dixon
P.O. Box 336
Crete, IL 60417
708/672-8682

Sue Dodge
Capital Church
7903 Westpark Drive
McLean, VA 22102
703/760-8888

Ann Downing
Downing Ministries
P.O. Box 767
Hendersonville, TN 37077
615/822-1900

Pat Duncan
P.O. Box 458
Circleville, OH 43113-0458
614/474-8896

Jeff and Sheri Easter
2429 Washington Highway
Lincolnton, GA 30817
615/385-5700

Barbara Fairchild
P.O. Box 1693
Branson, MO 65615
417/336-4718

Fairfield Four
Lee Olsen, Manager
c/o Keith Case & Associates
59 Music Square West
Nashville, TN 37203
615/327-4646

The Florida Boys
Les Beasley, Manager
910 East Kingsfield Road
Cantonment, FL 32533

Larry Ford
2670 Jackson Street
Fort Myers, FL 33901-5064

Eldridge Fox
P.O. Box 2622
Asheville, NC 28802
704/254-5046

Deacon Freeman
P.O. Box 311
Rockey Face, GA 30740
706/278-5835

Danny Gaither
403 Park Avenue
Alexandria, IN 46001
317/724-3039

Joy Gardner
1903 21st Avenue, South
Nashville, TN 37212

The Happy Goodmans
Rick Goodman, Manager
P.O. Box 158778
Nashville, TN 37215
615/370-0777

Mrs. Rusty Goodman
P.O. Box 834
Madison, TN 37115
615/860-4265

Greater Vision
   Chris Allman
   Rodney Griffin
   Gerald Wolfe
P.O. Box 50
Nashville, TN 37202
615/327-2805

Hilton Griswold
P.O. Box 202
Plainfield, IL 60544
815/436-8200

John Hall
P.O. Box 820344
Ft. Worth, TX 76182
817/498-8725

Suzy Hamblen
P.O. Box 1937
Canyon Country, CA 91386

Nancy Harmon
P.O. Box 210369
Bedford, TX 76095
817/498-5683

Heaven Bound
Jeff Gibson
P.O. Box 40707
Nashville, TN 37204
615/385-5700

Joel Hemphill
3551 Dickerson Road
Nashville, TN 37207
615/865-7100

Jake Hess
7827 Kolven Cove
Columbus, GA 31909
706/569-5461

Lou Wills Hildreth
P.O. Box 271106
Houston, TX 77277
713/592-7105

Jim Hill
5916 Valleybrook Road
Middletown, OH 45044

Wayne Hilliard
P.O. Box 121173
Nashville, TN 37212
615/297-1620

The Hinsons
Ronny Hinson
142 8th Avenue North
Nashville, TN 37203
615/244-8800

Kenny Hinson
P.O. Box 447
Hendersonville, TN 37075

The Hoppers
Claude and Connie Hopper
2811 U.S. 220
Madison, NC 27075
910/548-2968

The Isaacs
131 McNelley Drive
LaFollette, TN 37766
615/566-8527, booking agent

Gordon Jensen
P.O. Box 100512
Nashville, TN 37210
615/451-0090

Bob and Jeannie Johnson
3227 Wiseman Drive
Charlotte, NC 28277
704/568-7312

Charles Johnson and The Revivers
Canaan Records
1011 16th Avenue South
Nashville, TN 37212
615/327-1240

The Kingmen Quartet
P.O. Box 2622
Asheville, NC 28802
704/254-5046

Lillie Knauls
P.O. Box 608062
Orlando, FL 32860
407/246-4782

Harold Lane
2028 Franklin Limestone Ct.
Nashville, TN 37217
615/361-8606

Eva Mae LeFevre
4545 River Parkway 7-F
Atlanta, GA 30339
404/952-5330

Mylon LeFevre
Mylon LeFevre Ministries
P.O. Box 1287
Marietta, GA 30061-1287
404/590-5900

Hovie Lister and the Statesmen
P.O. Box 15501
Atlanta, GA 30333
404/371-8992

Mosie Lister
c/o Lillenas Publishing Company
P.O. Box 419527
Kansas City, MO 64141

Mark Lowry
P.O. Box 50262
Nashville, TN 37205
910/887-8288

Jack Marshall
205/553-8621

The Martins
　Judy Martin
　Jonathan Martin
　Joyce McCollough
410 Ashley 271 Rd.
Hamburg, AR 71646
501/853-5819

Babbie Mason
1480-F Terrell Mill Road, Suite 291
Marietta, GA 30067
404/952-1443

McDuffs
    Roger McDuff
    Coleman McDuff
    John McDuff
    Loren Matthews
P.O. Box 190
Pasadena, TX 77501
713/487-6741

Gary McSpadden
McSpadden Music Group
P.O. Box 50
Nashville, TN 37202
615/321-3333

Chuck Millhuff
Millhuff Ministries
P.O. Box 160
Olathe, KS 66051
913/764-0000

Buddy Mullins
P.O. Box 445
LaVergne, TN 37086
615/793-7335

The Mullins
c/o Roger Mullins
P.O. Box 629
Stockbridge, GA 30281
615/385-5700

Naomi and The Segos
P.O. Box 269
Centerville, GA 31028
912/953-5261

Rex Nelon/The Nelons
P.O. Box 460
Smyrna, GA 30081
404/434-8181

Calvin Newton
P.O. Box 375
Lookout Mt.,TN 37350
706/398-2822

Doug Oldham
1600 Belfield Place
Lynchburg, VA 24503

Palmetta State Quartet
Jack Pittman
P.O. Box 1507
Greenville, SC 29602
803/246-3599

Ivan Parker
P.O. Box 346
Mount Juliet, TN 37122
615/383-9136/booking agent

Squire Parsons
P.O. Box 279
Leicester, NC 28748
704/683-9134

Janet Paschal
Janet Paschal Ministries
P.O. Box 2609
Reidsville, NC 27323
919/342-0236

Roy Pauley
1935 S. Conway Road, B-1
Orlando, FL 32812
407/382-6325

Glen Payne
The Cathedrals
P.O. Box 1512
Stow, OH 44224
615/851-4500

Chonda Pierce
c/o The Ward Group
P.O. Box 58067
Nashville, TN 37205
615/373-0033

Rosa Nell (Speer) Powell
The Speer Family
54 Music Square, West
Nashville, TN 37203
615/327-2728

Dottie Rambo
Rambo Evangelistic Association
P.O. Box 50478
Nashville, TN 37205
615/329-1777

David Reece
612 Fedders Drive
Madison, TN 37115

Mary Tom (Speer) Reid
Ben Speer Music
54 Music Square, West
Nashville, TN 37203
615/329-9999

David Ring
P.O. Box 1986
Orlando, FL 32802
407/648-5432

Mrs. Rosie (Betty) Rozell
P.O. Box 706
Trussville, AL 35173
205/856-2974

Henry and Hazel Slaughter
P.O. Box 126
Pleasant View, TN 37146
615/746-2307

Allison Durham Speer
c/o Brian Speer
54 Music Square, West
Nashville, TN 37203
615/329-3535

Ben Speer
Ben Speer Music
54 Music Square, West
Nashville, TN 37203
615/329-9999

Brock and Faye Speer
The Speer Family
54 Music Square, West
Nashville, TN 37203
615/327-2728

Kevin Spencer Family
2327 Holtz Road
Shelby, OH 44875
419/347-8474

The Stamps
　J. D. Sumner
　Ed Enoch
　Jennifer Enoch
　Ed Hill
　Rick Strickland
P.O. Box 150532
Nashville, TN 37215
615/383-2887

Gordon Stoker
The Jordanaires
P.O. Box 159014
Nashville, TN 37215
615/665-0622

Tanya Goodman-Sykes
P.O. Box 834
Madison, TN 37115
615/832-8404

Kirk Talley
P.O. Box 6568
Knoxville, TN 37914

Roger and Debra Talley
P.O. Box 1918
Morristown, TN 37816-1918
615/235-2916

Kelly Nelon Thompson
P.O. Box 460
Smyrna, GA 30081
404/434-8181

Joe Thrasher
681 County Road 438
Wilsonville, AL 35186

Jack Toney
209 Sparks Avenue
Boaz, AL 35957
205/593-5454

Wally Varner
1493 Avenue I, S.W.
Winter Haven, FL 33880
813/293-9516

The Weatherfords
Lily Weatherford
P.O. Box 116
Paoli, OK 73074-0116
405/484-7212

Daryl Williams
P.O. Box 833
Antioch, TN 37011
615/360-3989

George Younce
The Cathedrals
P.O. Box 1512
Stow, OH 44224
615/851-4500

TABLE OF CONTENTS

177.	A Newborn Feeling	18.	Moving Up to Gloryland
43.	At the Cross	78.	My God is Real
32.	Beyond the Gates	174.	My Home
202.	Beyond the Sunset	53.	My Jesus, I Love Thee
12.	Bigger Than Any Mountain	72.	No, Not One!
17.	Boundless Love	172.	O Happy Day
192.	Burdens are Lifted at Calvary	64.	On Jordan's Stormy Banks
4.	Crown Him King	98.	Over in the Gloryland
95.	Did You Ever Go Sailin'?	88.	Paradise Island
65.	Everybody's Gonna Have a Wonderful Time Up there	129.	Peace, Peace, Wonderful Peace
142.	Follow Me	132.	Rise Again
162.	Get Away, Jordan	81.	Room at the Cross for You
111.	Go, Tell It on the Mountains	124.	Saved by the Hands
21.	God Leads Us Along	144.	Shall We Gather at the River
193.	Grace Greater Than Our Sin	102.	Sinner's Plea
194.	Hallelujah to the Lamb	115.	Soon and Very Soon
122.	He Ain't Never Done Me Nothin' But Good	136.	Stand Up for What I Stand For
100.	He Bought My Soul at Calvary	116.	Sweeter as the Days Go By
130.	He'll Find a Way	140.	Sweeter Each Day
161.	Hear the Voice of My Beloved	84.	Take Me in the Lifeboat
50.	Heaven's Joy Awaits	156.	The Answer's on the Way
8.	I am Not Ashamed	86.	The Bible Told Me So
104.	I Believe in a Hill Called Mount Calvary	62.	The Blood-Bought Church
184.	I Believe in the Old Time Way	24.	The Happy Jubilee
44.	I Don't Belong	108.	The Heavenly Parade
38.	I Don't Want to Live No More Without Jesus	90.	The Holy Hills of Heaven Call Me
33.	I Heard About a Stone	22.	The Joy of Heaven
54.	I Just Steal Away and Pray	48.	The Longer I Serve Him
40.	I Lost It All to Find Everything	118.	The Love of God
180.	I Need No Mansion Here	80.	The Old Rugged Cross
168.	I Thank My Savior for It All	148.	The Sun's Coming Up
120.	I Want to Walk Just as Close as I Can	112.	There's Power in the Blood
26.	I'll Keep Walking in the King's Highway	92.	Thread of Hope
196.	I'll Leave it All Behind	152.	Time Has Made a Change
126.	I'm Bound for that City	113.	Wait Till You See Me in My New Home
170.	I'm Free Again	76.	Waiting for His Return
97.	In the Garden	158.	We Have This Moment
37.	Jesus is All the World to Me	150.	We Shall Behold Him
2.	Lead Me to the Rock	73.	We Shall See Jesus
189.	Led Out of Bondage	106.	We've Come This Far by Faith
34.	Let's All Go Down to the River	134.	Welcome Home, My Child
60.	Let's Have a Revival	145.	What A Lovely Name
56.	Life Will be Sweeter Someday	200.	When All of God's Singers Get Home
182.	Lord, I'm Ready Now to Go	128.	When I Make My Last Move
29.	Moses, Take Your Shoes Off	68.	When I Meet You
82.	Move That Mountain	6.	When Morning Sweeps the Eastern Sky
		14.	When We All Get Together with the Lord
		47.	When You Pray
		138.	Won't It be Glory There?
		49.	Written in Red